Wasted

on

Jesus

Reaching for the Lover of Your Soul

JIM W. GOLL

Destiny Image® Publishers, Inc.
P.O. Box 310
Shippensburg, PA 17257-0310

"Speaking to the Purposes of God for This Generation
and for the Generations to Come"

ISBN 0-7684-2103-9

For Worldwide Distribution
Printed in the U.S.A.

This book and all other Destiny Image, Revival Press, MercyPlace, Fresh Bread, and Treasure House books are available at Christian bookstores and distributors worldwide.

For a U.S. bookstore nearest you, call **1-800-722-6774**.
For more information on foreign distributors, call **717-532-3040**.
Or reach us on the Internet: **http://www.reapernet.com**

Acknowledgment and Dedication

Every new book is like having another child! It truly is a work of love. It is conceived in intimacy with the Lord Himself, prayed over by hundreds, watched by many, coached by a few. Then there is the actual labor, and I do mean labor—the awkward transition moment that only a few know about, and then the final great push! Then you pick a name—oh, but the name! Hopefully you will enjoy this new baby—*Wasted on Jesus*. It is always a team effort.

I continue to thank the Lord for the consecration and graciousness of the Destiny Image staff. What a blessing they have been and continue to be to Michal Ann and me and our team at Ministry to the Nations. A bushel of thanks goes specifically to Don Nori, Sr. and to Don Milam for sticking with us. Thank you for your patience and covenant nature of the Lord. A big "high five" goes to Elizabeth Allen and Steve Nance for their scores of hours and diligent efforts in nursing this project along just us though it were their baby too.

An old gospel song starts off, "How can I say thanks…." That is how I feel about this birthing. The past and present staff of Ministry to the Nations continue to be sacrificial and supportive in every one of our projects. From the office staff, to the Prayer Shield warriors, to our directors and all those who partner with us—I could not do any of this without you.

I also want to thank the pioneers who have gone before me and those whom I have had the pleasure of walking beside. The teachings and writings of Mike Bickle, Don Nori, Sr., Dr. Steve Meeks, Derek Prince, Tommy Tenney, David Runcorn, Richard Foster, Mahesh

Chavda, Dr. Mark and Patti Virkler and Pat Gastineau in particular—you have helped to shape my world. The writings of some from the past such as Andrew Murray, Arthur Wallis, Charles Spurgeon, Francois Fenelon, St. Teresa, and so many others—what a blessing it is to walk in their shadow!

Lastly, I want to thank my dear family. Michal Ann—you are one of the best Christians I have ever met. Justin—your wit, wisdom and creativity have surpassed me. GraceAnn—your leadership skills with sensitivity are unfolding. Tyler—you are the best hugger on planet Earth! Rachel—your prayers and kisses mean so much to me. I truly want to say to my family—thanks for bearing with me, fighting with me on this project and wanting this book to be all that it could be. We did it!

I want to dedicate this book to the Lord Jesus Himself! Jesus, I really do want to waste my life on You! You are the Lover of my soul—how I long for Your courts and to enter into Your presence. I am a ruined man because You first loved me! Thank you, Jesus!

Blessings to each of you as you reach for the Lover of your soul!

Jim W. Goll

Endorsements

The new move of the Holy Spirit is about intimacy with God the Father and His Son, Jesus Christ. All of us who have begun to experience the joys of soaking in His presence during this new outpouring of the Spirit will appreciate Jim Goll's powerful work, *Wasted on Jesus*. It helps you move past common barriers to the continuous experience of the power of His great love. If you've been crying out, "More, Lord," this book is the answer to your prayers!

Melinda Fish
Author, *The River Is Here*
Editor, *Spread the Fire* magazine
Toronto Airport Christian Fellowship

In *Wasted on Jesus*, Jim Goll touches the very core of both the Father's heart and the Church's need in this hour—intimacy with Christ. Jim knows what it means to abide in "face to face" communion with the Master and has given us a most eloquent teaching on cultivating that communion.

Steven Fry
President, Messenger Fellowship
Author, *I AM: The Unveiling of God*

As I read a book, I look for the life of the Lord in experience and expression through the author. I honestly have more information than I can presently digest. The Church at large is inundated with clouds of information, while the heart of the Church languishes in need of experiencing the realities of God. We need to move out of the shadowy places of religion into vibrant union with the Lord himself.

Don't read this book to gain more information—read it with eager anticipation for an "adventure of the heart"! The Lord makes Himself very attractive through the pages of this book! Open up your heart to be affected by His love, incited in your pursuit and compelled forward in the upward call of God in Christ Jesus. Having known Jim Goll for years, I appreciate the "search" in his heart to experience God personally and then express Him to the world.

Pat Gastineau
Word of Love Ministries

Devout believers hunger to experience spiritual intimacy with Jesus. They hunger for someone to lead out them out of the bondage of rationalism and into a full encounter with the Holy Spirit. *Wasted on Jesus* helps meet this hunger by offering spiritual intimacy through contemplative Christian experience.

Mark Virkler
President, Christian Leadership University

Jim Goll has greatly impacted my life through his teachings and ministry of prayer. In your hands is a tool that will challenge you to waste your life on God! Read it and you too will catch the fire and passion to pour your all out for our Lord Jesus !

Lou Engle
Author, *Digging the Wells of Revival* and *Fast Forward*
Director of the Elijah Revolution

Many believers are longing for a contemplative dimension to be added to their faith. We can find God in the world around us as manifest, in the world above us as transcendent, and in the world within us as immanent. It is this inner world which Jim Goll explores in this marvelous book. I believe one of the Holy Spirit's agendas for this hour is calling the Church to find the Christ who dwells within. This intimate and more organic relationship with God is the heartbeat of this book. If you are hungry to know the indwelling Christ in a deeper way, then *Wasted on Jesus* will be an inspiring guide.

Steven Meeks
Senior pastor
Calvary Community Church, Houston, TX

Jim Goll is one of those special "wasted" gifts to the Body of Christ. His prophetic insight and extreme pursuit of God are contagious. This book, *Wasted on Jesus*, is a must for every believer who is not satisfied with the status quo of church life and wants to be called God's friend.

Bart Pierce
Author, *Seeking Our Brothers*

If you are looking for a book that will usher you into God's presence—this is it! *Wasted on Jesus* reveals the heart of Jesus flowing through the pen of Jim Goll. It is must reading for every Christian who is searching for a deeper and more intimate walk with the Lord.

Elizabeth (Beth) Alves
Co-founder and President
Intercessors International

Contents

Foreword

This thing called Christianity is all about our glorious Christ Jesus and His passionate pursuit to find volunteer lovers of God whom He transforms to become deliverers of men. We love God because He first loved us! In turn, as we are given a glimpse of the transcendent majesty of Christ, we can't help but pour our lives out to Him as a sacrificial drink offering. He is altogether lovely! But a mystery exists—through the rose colored lens of the blood of the Lamb, the Father thinks we are altogether lovely as well!

Over the past twenty plus years, I have personally had the privilege of being involved in public intercessory gatherings on almost a daily basis. Now as I serve as the Director of the International House of Prayer in the greater Kansas City area, my heart is encouraged to see many people becoming infected with the desire to be Marys of Bethany and Annas of the Temple. Yes, the golden bowls on His altar in heaven will be filled with our prayers and praise until they are overflowing with our extravagant acts of divine romance. He is worth it, isn't He?

This latest book by Jim Goll will help you in the process of keeping the fire of God burning brightly on the altar of your heart. It will inspire you to devote yourself to Him—not out of religious arm twisting—but out of a passionate yearning for the Son of God Himself. As you read *Wasted on Jesus*, may you be encouraged to give Christ Jesus your all. And may you find that communion with God is more than a ritual or spiritual discipline—it is what you were created for!

Join Jim Goll and me and a growing throng of others in simply seeking to lavishly give our hearts to Him as he has given His to us! As you read this book, may you too be consumed with the fire of His love!

Mike Bickle
Director, International House of Prayer of Kansas City

Introduction

A radical desire is arising across the global Body of Christ from people who just want to waste their lives on Jesus! They are not satisfied with things as they currently are in their lives or in the corporate Church. These desperate souls are crying out to the Lord for mentors, training, and insight to help them walk farther down the road themselves. They want to know Jesus! In Church history past, these mentors were often called "masters" or "spiritual guides." Where are these tutors for today's discontent Christian populace?

In my own life, books have played a great part in my process of becoming. Books have often been mentors, guides, and teachers to me. That is why I have been pouring so much of my life in these past few years into writing training materials, study guides, and books. I would love to come and sit with you—but obviously, I am just one person. However, I can come into your living room through the vehicle of a book. That is why I have written *Wasted on Jesus*. I want to come sit with you in your own home and have a fireside chat with you!

I want to see you grow in Christ. Now, God knows I have not arrived yet! But one thing I am committed to is giving away what I have been given. That is actually one of the Kingdom principles of increase for yourself—give and it shall be given! So here we are—another round of vintage material I have learned and am learning from my tutor the Holy Spirit. He is a great teacher.

I want to see Jesus Christ receive the rewards of His suffering. I want to see a whole generation of Marys of Bethany, Annas of the temple, and Joshuas of meditation arise! Don't you? That is why you have picked up this "in your face" book with the glaring title of *Wasted on Jesus*. You can't think of a better thing you would like to do with your life than to pour it out as a drink offering before Him! Isn't that right?

This book takes you on another leg of my personal journey with the Lover of my soul. Once again, I feel like a spiritual archaeologist who is dusting off the relics of the past to bring them forth for the present. You will learn to love what is often called the "spiritual disciplines." I am presenting these life changing concepts not from a "works" mind-set, but from a heart that just aches to be joined in unison to sing one song with Him.

On the practical side, I have divided this book into three parts that are progressive in nature. In Part One, "The Inward Journey: Proceeding Into His Presence," we discover why Mary of Bethany would pour out her life's savings on her newfound Lord. Dusting off the truths of the past of contemplative prayer, we discover that it is a delight, not a burden. Then we probe a mystery—that *we* are the Father's House—and we discover what true communion requires.

Part Two is called "The Quietness of the Soul: Waiting on Him." In this section we take a stand to reclaim what is rightfully ours—that which the New Age movement and other groups have so badly distorted. We learn that quieting our soul before God is part of our Christian inheritance. We rediscover that He is our Shepherd and He wants to lead us by the quiet stream. We dust off the artifacts of biblical meditation and the lost arts of listening, waiting, and watching with our Messiah. We even dig deeper by looking into the reality of walking in union with Christ Jesus.

Part Three is termed "The Outward Journey: The Fire of His Love." Once we have learned to cultivate these spiritual graces, we find that we must do something with what we have just received or we might burn up! We now put feet to our love relationship with our Mentor by entering into the Bridegroom's fast. We allow Him to walk through our tabernacle to see whether there really is any fire burning on the altar of our heart. Then we are commissioned to go put the live coals of fire onto other people's lives.

One of my goals is help make you worse off than I am! What I mean is that I want to see you shake off complacency and get *Wasted on Jesus*! If you hunger for more of God and less of you—then this book was written just for you.

Now, take your shoes off and let's sit down for awhile. I want to have a fireside chat with you. Together, let's keep reaching for the Lover of our soul!

With eager anticipation,
Jim W. Goll

Part One
The Inward Journey: Proceeding Into His Presence

Chapter One

Wasted Worship?

Wasted! That pretty well sums up the lives of many people today. Whether it is wasted potential, wasted opportunity, or wasted time or money, it is a tragic reflection of a spiritually adrift and morally bankrupt culture in which everyday life for more and more people has become pointless, aimless, and hopeless. Like the prodigal son, a lot of folks seem to have no higher goal in life than to "waste [their] substance with riotous living."[1] They are regular "party animals," trying vainly to fill their empty lives by pursuing one cheap thrill or shallow pleasure after another. How many of us have heard a friend, an acquaintance, or a work colleague say something like, "I'm going to get totally wasted tonight!" By getting "wasted," of course, he means that he intends either to get falling-down drunk on booze or spaced out on his particular drug of choice (sometimes both).

Such widespread hedonism is a sign of our times. A fierce conflict is raging in our world today as the forces of evil square off against the forces of good. We are in an age of competing altars: demonic fire versus holy fire, worldly passion versus godly passion. Battle lines have been drawn, and the fight will only intensify as this end-time generation unfolds before us. As those in the stranglehold of the world get more and more "wasted" on sex, drugs, entertainment, and violence, another body of people is arising who are just as willingly and with just as much abandon getting "wasted" on Jesus!

These passionate, fiery radicals make up the first wave assault troops in this cosmic struggle to determine which "controlling substance" will rule our lives. They are the vanguard of a great army consumed with a mighty spiritual passion that is spreading across the worldwide body of Christ today. That passion is a craving that transcends sectarian and confessional lines, touching both men and women, young and old, "professional" ministers as well as every day believers in the Lord Jesus Christ. Multitudes of people yearn for closeness to God. They long to know Him the way Moses did, to whom God spoke "face to face, just as a man speaks to his friend."[2] For many of us, "church as usual" has failed to feed our deepest hunger. Old ways of "religion" do not quench our thirst. Man-made traditions with their dusty dogma, frayed formalism, and seemingly pointless patterns simply won't pass muster anymore. Every day, more and more anguished, Spirit-fueled cries for deeper intimacy rise to God from the famished hearts of His children.

God Wants Intimacy With Us

God has always wanted to be near His people. In the beginning, the first human couple enjoyed open, unbroken intimacy and fellowship with their Creator as they walked with Him "in the garden in the cool of the day."[3] As we all know, sin broke that relationship and erected a "veil" of separation between the holy God and His own creation. God wanted to be near us so much—to restore the breach— that He became one of us. Through His Son, Jesus Christ, He "became flesh, and dwelt among us...full of grace and truth."[4] By His death and resurrection, Christ tore away the veil and opened the way once more for face-to-face intimacy with the Father for everyone who will believe. Shortly before His death, Jesus told His disciples, "In My Father's house are many dwelling places; if it were not so, I would have told you; for I go to prepare a place for you. If I go and prepare a place for you, I will come again and receive you to Myself, that where I am, there you may be also."[5] God *wants* us to share intimate fellowship with Him in His house!

Personally, I hunger for a place called "home." As I travel from city to city and nation to nation, a yearning, puzzling question keeps rising up in my spirit: "Just where is home?"

An old proverb says, "Home is where the heart is." Yes, home is where intimate relationships are born and nurtured. Except for God, no one knows us better than the members of our own natural family. For most of us, home is where we can relax and be ourselves, where we can "let our hair down" and, in the words of my generation, "let it all hang out." This is the kind of fellowship God wants us to have with Him. It is also the kind of intimacy that more and more Christians today are yearning for. By and large, much of the modern Church has failed to deliver on its promise of a meaningful relationship with God, offering up rigid ritual, shallow formality, and empty tradition as cheap substitutes.

Why Is Intimacy With God So Hard to Find?

If spiritual intimacy is such a high priority for God and such a longing in the hearts of countless believers, why does it seem to be so elusive? Why do so many Christians fail to experience the kind of closeness to God they crave? One reason may be spiritual laziness. We would rather have the blessings of God handed to us on a silver platter than to have to put forth any effort of our own. Intimacy with God is not automatic; it takes time and commitment, motivated by a ravishing hunger for Him. I am convinced, however, that there is another, more significant reason. Many of us don't draw close to God because we plain don't know how. Cultivating a radical, intimate relationship with God is virtually a lost art to believers today. We want everything "right now." Somewhere along the way we have developed very short spiritual attention spans. We rush into our "time with God," rattle off our list of requests, then rush off again. It's rather like shopping for the bare necessities to get by and never realizing that God has prepared a banquet for us and is waiting for us to sit down and enjoy it! We must learn to take the time to get to *know* Him as He knows us.

I have often wondered who Jesus regarded as His "bosom buddies." We know that during His earthly ministry Jesus enjoyed several close ministry relationships, but did He have any real *friends*? I believe He did. Among the twelve apostles, Peter, James, and John comprised an "inner circle" with whom Jesus was particularly close. Outside the apostolic group, one of His warmest relationships was with a trio of siblings from the village of Bethany: a man named Lazarus and his sisters, Martha and Mary. Let's look in on them.

"Lord, If You Had Been Here..."

Jesus, therefore, six days before the Passover, came to Bethany where Lazarus was, whom Jesus had raised from the dead. So they made Him a supper there, and Martha was serving; but Lazarus was one of those reclining at the table with Him. Mary then took a pound of very costly perfume of pure nard, and anointed the feet of Jesus and wiped His feet with her hair; and the house was filled with the fragrance of the perfume.[6]

Try to frame this picture clearly in your mind. Here is Lazarus, whom Jesus recently had raised from the dead, "reclining at the table with Him" in a contemplative frame of mind. How would *you* feel if, like Lazarus, you had been all the way to death and back? John relates the story in the 11th chapter of his Gospel. Lazarus was very sick and his sisters sent for Jesus. By the time Jesus arrived with His disciples, after a deliberate delay of two days, Lazarus was already dead and had been in the grave four days. Wrapped in a linen shroud, his body had been tucked away in a dark sepulcher with a giant stone rolled across the entrance. It was past time for a healing; Lazarus was dead! It was past time even for a miracle; after four days in the tomb his corpse would stink from decay.

As He so often did, Jesus appeared on the scene apparently late, but in reality just in time. Immediately the sisters confronted Him, their hearts brimming over with the hurt and confusion they felt at being let down by Someone with whom they shared such a deep bond. "Lord, if You had been here, my brother would not have died."[7] Behind their words lay the implied rebuke, "Lord, if You had come *when we first sent for You*, Lazarus would still be alive." Such honesty comes only from a relationship of transparency. Although Jesus wept over Lazarus' death and the sorrow of the sisters, He had a greater plan in mind than just healing a sick friend. With the piercing words "Lazarus, come forth," Jesus raised the dead man, revealed the awesome power of God, and brought glory to His Father.

Now, sometime later, this same Lazarus is "reclining at the table" with Jesus. Imagine the wonder and the power of that moment. Lazarus didn't immediately rush out and kick off his "Lazarus Resurrection Holy Ghost Campaign." Instead, he quietly reclined at the table with His Lord and Friend. It seems as though these guys simply enjoyed "hanging out" together. Apparently, they had missed each other's company. Maybe there were notes to compare from having been on the other side!

As Jesus and his friend Lazarus reclined at supper, "Martha was serving." Here is Martha—solid, dependable Martha—a devoted servant who most often expressed her love through practical acts of service in meeting the physical needs of her Master and Friend. This is the same Martha who on another occasion got so caught up in her busyness that she complained to Jesus that her sister Mary wasn't pulling her weight.

> "Lord, do You not care that my sister has left me to do all the serving alone? Then tell her to help me." But the Lord answered and said to her, "Martha, Martha, you are worried and bothered about so many things; but only one thing is necessary, for Mary has chosen the good part, which shall not be taken away from her."[8]

Extravagant Love

This brings us around to Mary. Here is dear, sweet Mary; Mary the penitent, Mary the lover. The "good part" she chose was to sit at the feet of her Lord and Friend, rapt in His words and His holy Presence. Now, as her brother Lazarus reclines at table with Jesus and as her sister Martha serves, Mary takes a more demonstrative approach. In an act of breath-taking extravagance she lavishes her love on Jesus in a display of unbridled devotion and abandoned worship. "Mary then took a pound of very costly perfume of pure nard, and anointed the feet of Jesus and wiped His feet with her hair; and the house was filled with the fragrance of the perfume."[9]

What else do we know about this Mary of Bethany and the circumstances surrounding her extraordinary display of extravagant love? According to the parallel accounts recorded in the Gospels of Matthew and Mark, this supper on Jesus' behalf was held in the Bethany home of a man known as "Simon the leper."[10] Luke's account further identifies Simon as a Pharisee.[11] Although some biblical scholars contend that the story related in Matthew, Mark, and Luke is a similar but separate event from the story recorded in John, it is possible that all four accounts are different versions of the same event. John's account, however, is the only one that identifies Mary by name; the other gospel writers refer to her simply as "a woman." Luke goes a little further, identifying her as a "sinner."[12] In that context the word "sinner" (Gr. *hamartolos*) refers specifically to an immoral woman, or a woman of ill repute. Matthew and Mark record that she poured the perfume on Jesus' head[13], while Luke and John say that she poured it on His feet, adding the additional detail that she wiped His feet with her hair.[14] We know from the different accounts that Jesus' disciples as well as others were in attendance and witnessed Mary's radical and controversial act.

Let's try to consolidate these various accounts and see if we can frame the complete picture. Jesus is in Bethany, the village where Lazarus, Martha, and Mary live. While there, He attends a supper at the invitation of and in the home of a Pharisee known as Simon the leper. Lazarus is also one of the dinner guests, as are Jesus' disciples and others, perhaps some of Simon's friends. Martha is there to serve. It appears that this was not a small, intimate meal but rather a large dinner party. Suddenly, in the middle of everything, Mary appears, carrying an ornate bottle of very expensive perfume. Seemingly oblivious to the presence of perhaps two dozen or more witnesses, she stands behind Jesus' feet, wetting them with her tears.[15] Breaking open the vial of perfume, Mary first anoints Jesus' head, and then His feet. Then, kneeling down, she gently and lovingly wipes Jesus' feet with her hair.

Such a blatantly public display of intimate affection probably caused a sudden embarrassed silence from everyone else in the room. For some, that embarrassed silence quickly became shocked outrage, but Mary just flat didn't care. She was deeply in love with a Man—a Messiah—who had forgiven her and saved her, and treated her with a love, dignity, and respect that no one else had ever afforded her. Whatever else she may once have been or done, no matter how she may have wasted her life before, she is different now. Jesus has changed her. Now Mary is bent on wasting her life on her Lord—the God who loved her and forgave her—and she doesn't care who knows about it or what anyone else thinks. She has eyes only for Him. For Mary, the expensive perfume means nothing; it is merely a symbol of the unrestrained love she feels in her spirit and of her determination from that day forward to waste her life on God.

"Why Has This Perfume Been Wasted?"

It didn't take long for Mary's radical expression of love for Jesus to provoke pretty strong criticism.

> But Judas Iscariot, one of His disciples, who was intending to betray Him, said, "Why was this perfume not sold for three hundred denarii, and given to poor people?" Now he said this, not because he was concerned about the poor, but because he was a thief, and as he had the money box, he used to pilfer what was put into it. Therefore Jesus said, "Let her alone, so that she may keep it for the day of My burial. For you always have the poor with you, but you do not always have Me."[16]

Matthew's and Mark's versions are essentially identical; let's see what Mark says.

> *But some were indignantly remarking to one another, "Why has this perfume been wasted? For this perfume might have been sold for over three hundred denarii, and the money given to the poor." And they were scolding her. But Jesus said, "Let her alone; why do you bother her? She has done a good deed to Me. For you always have the poor with you, and whenever you wish you can do good to them; but you do not always have Me. She has done what she could; she has anointed My body beforehand for the burial. Truly I say to you, wherever the gospel is preached in the whole world, what this woman has done will also be spoken of in memory of her."*[17]

The essential difference here is that in John's account, Judas Iscariot voices the criticism, while Mark simply says that "some were indignantly remarking." Matthew specifically states that "the disciples were indignant."[18] It is safe to say that a chorus of scandalized voices arose, with Judas perhaps as the "lead singer." On the surface, the criticism appears quite practical and "religiously correct." The perfume was worth "three hundred denarii," equivalent in those days to a *year's wages* for a common laborer. I have often wondered where and how Mary acquired so much money. Did she earn it? Was the perfume a gift? At any rate, why "waste" such valuable essence on one person (no matter who He was) in a matter of a few seconds?

This is the typical response of "religious" people when confronted with an act of genuine spiritual devotion; it is incomprehensible to them.[19] The religious mind counts the cost of such extravagance and concludes that it is a waste. Such criticism is almost always clothed in pious garb: "This perfume might have been *sold*…and the money given to the poor." What religious critics fail to understand is that extravagant acts of abandoned, "wasted" worship that are motivated by unfettered love for God need no justification or explanation before men. In fact, as I study "the Book," I find that extravagance in worship *always* wins out with God over self-conscious conservatism. The real issue is whether we are trying to *give* attention or *gain* attention. God looks at the heart and welcomes the open, unfeigned adoration of His children, however it is expressed.

This is why Jesus jealously rose to Mary's defense. God is jealous for His glory and for His children. "Let her alone, so that she may keep it for the day of My burial. For you always have the poor with you, but you do not always have Me."[20] He cut right through the pious hypocrisy to focus on matters of the heart. What is the true object of our love? Jesus said that wherever a man's treasure is, that is where his heart will be also.[21] Mary's heart was in the right place, and Jesus affirmed her. Once again, Mary had "chosen the good part," and it would not be taken away from her. She wasted everything she had ever achieved or earned on her new Lord!

"Do You See This Woman?"

In Luke's account of this story Jesus asks Simon the Pharisee a searching question.

> Now when the Pharisee who had invited Him saw this, he said to himself, "If this man were a prophet He would know who and what sort of person this woman is who is touching Him, that she is a sinner."…Turning toward the woman, [Jesus] said to Simon, "Do you see this woman? I entered your house; you gave Me no water for My feet, but she has wet My feet with her tears and wiped them with her hair. You gave Me no kiss; but she, since the time I came in, has not ceased to kiss My feet. You did not anoint My head with oil, but she anointed My feet with perfume. For this reason I say to you, her sins, which are many, have been forgiven, for she loved much; but he who is forgiven little, loves little."[22]

Jesus asked Simon, "Do you see this woman?" If I were to answer for Simon I would say that he did *not* see her. Oh, Simon knew she was in the room and he knew *who* she was and *what* she was, but he never really *saw her.* Jesus did. He saw past her natural, outward appearance, the "wrapper" we all come in, and gazed straight into her heart. He looked beyond who and what she was to who and what she *could be.* Probably no one but Jesus had ever regarded Mary that highly, and she loved Him for it.

Jesus chided his host for his failure to provide the customary hospitalities of the day—water for washing dusty, smelly feet, a kiss of greeting, and oil to cleanse the sweat and grime of the road—but that was beside the point. Jesus wasn't concerned about social amenities; He was concerned with love, gratitude, and worship. What Simon had failed to offer Mary provided in abundance. Jesus wanted Simon to understand that the issue is not the presence or absence of outward actions or traditions, but the inward condition of the heart. Those who have been forgiven much love much; those who have been forgiven little love little. As a religious Pharisee, Simon likely had little sense of awareness of his need for forgiveness, and therefore little sense either of the love of God or of compassion for those who, in his eyes, were worse "sinners" than he was. Simon had little love for Jesus, and it showed in his actions (or lack of them).

What Is Different About Mary?

Mary was a different story. She knew the depth of her sinful past and the depth of the forgiveness she had received from the Lord. Now she was ready to give everything she had, even her very self, to be poured out and wasted on Him just like the perfume she had "wasted" in anointing his head and feet, the fragrance of which permeated the room.

No one knows for sure what Mary's earlier life was like, but as a "sinner" or woman of ill repute, she probably had a great deal of knowledge and experience on how to "approach" and attract a man. She probably knew just how to wear her hair, just how to dress, exactly what perfume to wear, and the precise moves to make and looks to give that would catch a man's eye (and his coin purse).

That night in Bethany, Mary may have approached Jesus, a strong, virile, Jewish man in his early thirties, in a manner similar to the way she had approached many others, at least *outwardly*. She came to Him, "let her hair down" and proceeded to wipe His feet. Certainly, with her reputation, such an act would have appeared to those looking on as sensual in the extreme. Mary's actions probably would have aroused all sorts of thoughts and desires in the hearts of the average men of her day. But this time was different; Mary knew it and Jesus knew it.

Perhaps many men had touched her sexually—men who had used her or abused her; men who had *wanted* her but did not really want *her*. Some of these same men might have even been in the room watching with bated breath to see what would follow. But this time was different. No one had ever touched Mary the way Jesus had—in her inmost being. Many men had looked at Mary with lustful eyes. No one had ever looked at her the way Jesus did. Everything about her was exposed to His penetrating gaze—her pain, her guilt, her shame, her longing to know true love. All of these found relief and fulfillment in Him. More importantly, Jesus saw Mary's inner beauty crying to be released. He forgave her and set her free. When Jesus *saw* Mary as she was, Mary saw Jesus as He was—Master, Lord, Savior, the Lover of her soul—and she had eyes for no one else anymore.

Wasting Our Fragrance

The longer I walk with the Lord, the more I realize how great a sinner I am. I become more aware of how far away from Him I have been and, in some senses, still am. At the same time, the more I walk with Him the more I realize how approachable He is. As we realize more and more who we are as sinners and as we recognize the magnitude of what Christ has done for us, the more our hearts will rise up in us like the heart of Mary of Bethany. We'll find ourselves saying, "Lord, I want my life to be a drink offering poured out upon You."

I'm tired of boring church and mundane Christianity; how about you? But please realize, if church is boring and mundane, it's our fault because we *are* the church. Each of us is just as close to God as we want to be. He is always there, ready to draw us deeper. Oh, how I want to pour out my life as a drink offering before Him! As for me and my house, I want to waste my life on Jesus! Want to join me?

The revelation of forgiveness and righteousness freely given to us by Christ results in radical, authentic worship. But we need to learn to be quiet before the Lord, to take a little time to let the tears of our hearts pour out to Him. Each of us has a unique and precious fragrance that only we can give to be "wasted" upon our Messiah. The one who has been forgiven much loves much. How much have *you* been forgiven? What fragrance can you pour out in honor of the King of kings? Someone else may think that your particular fragrance "stinks"; you might feel the same way about mine. What's important is that we take what we have and "waste" it on the Lord. No matter what others may think of our "fragrance," when we pour it out as a love offering to God it becomes in His nostrils a sweet-smelling incense, not only acceptable, but greatly desired and longed for!

The Door to Greater Intimacy

Wasting our life on God is a doorway to greater intimacy with Him. It is a lifestyle practice that has been sorely missing in the modern, "fast-food" church for many, many years. It's beginning to make a comeback, however. Hungry believers in all parts of the world and in every stream and denomination are starting to rediscover this lost key to the simple, deeper life. The Lord Himself is stirring it up and bringing it to the remembrance and awareness of His people. He is raising up a company of friends, a society of the broken-hearted, yet grateful.

This is neither a gender issue nor a theological, doctrinal, or sectarian issue, but an issue of the heart; a heart overflowing with love and gratitude to the One who poured out and "wasted" His divine fragrance on us. What greater "waste" could there be but that "while we were yet sinners, Christ died for us"?[23]

God is drawing and calling His people to a deeper, focused walk with Him, not just into the inner court but all the way into the Most Holy Place, that safe, quiet inner chamber to which He alone has the key. But He has given us the key and has invited us to come in.

Jesus said, "But you, when you pray, go into your inner room, close your door and pray to your Father who is in secret, and your Father who sees what is done in secret will reward you."[24] Our prayers are welcomed and received before Him just as Jesus welcomed and received Mary's tears that wetted His feet and her perfume that anointed His body for burial. Like Mary, a people of God are arising whose chief goal will be to waste their lives on Him.

Letting Our Hair Down

Not long ago I was in a meeting with Thetus Tenney, Tommy Tenney's mother. Thetus Tenney is a wonderful, God fearing and godly woman. I know now why Tommy carries God's presence the way he does; he has had excellent forerunners, not just his father and grandfather, but also his mother.

On this occasion I had a prophetic word involving Thetus Tenney. Having lived so many years in the Pentecostal tradition, she still publicly wears her hair in a nice, neat, tight bun. It's a good thing she likes me, "messer-upper" that I am, or I probably wouldn't have gotten away with this. I had several other people there purposefully watching so that it would be pure. I walked up to her and said, "What I am about to do I have never done before and will probably never do again, but I'm going to do a prophetic action right now." I took the pin out of her hair and let down her flowing gray, beautiful, thick mane. It was quite long and came way down her back. Then I said, "God is going to untie the knot in the Church, and He is going to teach us how to let down our hair in His presence. We will be like Mary of Bethany and it will be a sacrifice pleasing to our Messiah." Thetus didn't mind this at all, for she too is a "Mary" who has poured her life out before her Lord.

A key to living a life wasted on God is to learn to enter into the place of quietness before God; a place of meditation and what many writers of old have called contemplative prayer. That is where true intimacy and spiritual communion reach their fullest realization.

An Invitation Into His Presence

I invite you and challenge you to go on a journey with me to that secret inner place, a life wasted on Jesus. It is an invitation to join the society of the broken-hearted, a people of gratitude, meekness, and faith who have felt the warm gaze of the Lord into their inmost being and have heard His affirmation, "I knew you were like that all the time." Out of that brokenness will come forth a fragrance that will fill the house, the fragrance of abandoned, "wasted worship" and a life completely poured out for God. That fragrance will rise and be collected in Heaven, where one day the Messiah himself will be pleased to pour it back out as an ointment to draw His people to himself and bring healing to the nations. Then each of us will return to the place of a little child, at rest and composed, having sucked at the breast of God.

The road to true intimacy with God is an inward journey, proceeding into His Presence through the entrance gate of quietness of the soul. It is a narrow track that lies well off the beaten path, virtually unseen and ignored by the vast majority of humanity careening headlong through life. Although it is not easy to find, the riches and rewards are well worth the effort. Why don't you come along with me? Let's set off on a trek down a road less traveled. Along the way we will meet other bold explorers who have gone before us, and refresh ourselves at the wellsprings of their wisdom and insight. May the adventure that awaits us whet your appetite to get "wasted" on Jesus!

Reflection Questions

1. What does the word *wasted* mean to you?
2. Why did the observers mock Mary of Bethany as she lavishly wasted her life's earnings on the Lord?
3. How does God respond to extravagant worship?

Recommended Reading

God's Favorite House by Tommy Tenney (Destiny Image, 1999)
Worship: The Pattern of Things in Heaven by Joseph Garlington (Destiny Image, 1997)
I AM: The Unveiling of God by Steve Fry (Multnomah, 2000)

Endnotes

1. Lk. 15:13b, KJV.
2. Ex. 33:11.
3. Gen. 3:8.
4. Jn. 1:14.
5. Jn. 14:2-3.
6. Jn. 12:1-3.
7. Jn. 11:21, 32.
8. Lk. 10:40-42.
9. Jn. 12:3.
10. Mt. 26:6; Mk. 14:3.
11. Lk. 7:36, 39.
12. Lk. 7:37.
13. Mt. 26:7, Mk. 14:3.
14. Lk. 7:38, Jn. 12:3.
15. Lk. 7:38.
16. Jn. 12:4-8.
17. Mk. 14:4-9.
18. Mt. 26:8.
19. I use the word "religious" here to refer to the "spirit of religion," a false spirituality that knows nothing of a personal relationship with the living God, but only empty form, tradition, and ritual. "Religious" people in this sense are those who, in the words of the apostle Paul, have "a form of godliness, although they have denied its power" (2 Tim. 3:5).
20. Jn. 12:7-8.
21. Mt. 6:21.
22. Lk. 7:39, 44-47.
23. Rom. 5:8.
24. Mt. 6:6.

Chapter Two

The Road to True Intimacy

C an you imagine what it must have been like to know Jesus in the flesh, to walk with Him, talk with Him, and see His face on a daily basis as His disciples did? How did it feel to watch Him heal a blind man with mud made from dirt and spit, or cleanse a leper with a gentle touch, or raise the dead with a word of command? What was it like to live with Him day in and day out, to see Him both when He was full of energy and when He was dog-tired, when He was full of the joy of the Spirit and when He grieved over the rejection and unbelief of the very people He came to save? How did it feel to sit at His feet and hear the greatest truth and wisdom ever spoken by human lips? What was it like to recline at table with Jesus when He said, "This is My body which is given for you...This cup which is poured out for you is the new covenant in My blood"?[1] How did it feel to love Him—and then watch Him die?

Leaning on the Breast of Jesus

Only a very few people were privileged to know Jesus on such personal and intimate terms as these. John was one of them. This "beloved" apostle, along with his brother James and Simon Peter, comprised the "inner circle" of Jesus' closest friends. In the Gospel and the epistles which bear his name, John himself hinted at the intimacy of his relationship with Jesus. During the Last Supper, "There was reclining on Jesus' bosom one of His disciples, whom Jesus loved."[2] Bible scholars generally agree that John is referring to himself. "Reclining on Jesus' bosom" is a beautiful description of intimacy in friendship and fellowship! Four other times in his Gospel John refers to himself as the "disciple whom Jesus loved."[3]

John also opens his first epistle with a reference to his firsthand knowledge of Jesus.

> *What was from the beginning, what we have heard, what we have seen with our eyes, what we have looked at and touched with our hands, concerning the Word of Life...what we have seen and heard we proclaim to you also, so that you too may have fellowship with us; and indeed our fellowship is with the Father, and with His Son Jesus Christ.*[4]

These are the words of a man who knew Jesus intimately and personally. John speaks of Jesus as One whom he had *heard* with his own ears, *seen* with his own eyes, and *touched* with his own hands. As a result, John enjoys *fellowship* with the *Father, and with His Son Jesus Christ*, and he wants his readers (including us) to enjoy *that same fellowship*!

How do we enjoy intimate fellowship with Jesus, who is no longer physically present, or with the Father, who is Spirit? Our fellowship comes in and through the Holy Spirit, who communes with our spirit as children of God. Part of the Holy Spirit's role in our lives is to bring us into intimate fellowship with Christ. In order for that to happen, we must first learn to calm our own spirit and still our inmost being.

If We Want to Be Intimate, We Must Learn to Be Still

We cannot fully realize true intimacy with God until we learn how to come before Him in quietness of spirit, mind, and body. An atmosphere of stillness is absolutely essential for us if we wish to experience deep, loving communion with our Lord. David the psalmist wrote, "My soul waits in silence for God only."[5] The prophet Habakkuk proclaimed, "But the Lord is in His holy temple. Let all the earth be silent before Him."[6] When Elijah listened for the counsel of God, he heard the Lord not in the wind, the earthquake, or the fire, but in "a still small voice."[7] In the 46th psalm the Lord calls on us to "Be still, and know that I am God."[8]

This "knowing" goes far beyond mere informational knowledge. The Hebrew word *yada* is used for all types of knowledge, including the most intimate relationships. It is the same word used in the phrase, "And Adam knew Eve his wife." To "know" God in this sense means to have His Spirit infilling us, His breath inspiring us, and His heart invigorating us. "Knowing" God means to be brought into vital, personal union with Jesus Christ our Lord. That's the kind of intimacy He seeks with us, but entering into it requires quietness of spirit on our part.

Unfortunately, our society does not encourage or prepare us for quietness. We are surrounded daily by a bedlam of competing voices—both good and evil—that constantly clamor for our attention. If we don't know how to listen, the "still small voice" of God can easily be drowned in the din.

Quietness is neither a new discovery nor a recent innovation. It is not even a new slant on an old discovery. Quietness is a time honored and proven method of prayer and fellowship with God that is almost totally ignored by modern-day Christians. Learning to be quiet before the Lord is one of the greatest challenges we face today in our quest to enter in and experience true intimacy with Him.

Stillness Is a Great Challenge, but It Brings Great Rewards

In their powerful book *Communion with God*, Mark and Patti Virkler speak both of the importance of quietness to intimacy with God and the challenge of achieving it.

> If we are going to commune with God, first we must become still. Habakkuk went to his guard post to pray (Hab. 2:1). In the early morning when it was still dark, Jesus departed to a lonely place to pray (Mk. 1:35). And after a day's ministry, Jesus went to a mountain to pray.
>
> In order for our inner man to commune with God, we must **first** remove external distractions. We must find a place where we can be alone and undisturbed, so that we can center down into our hearts without being distracted by our external circumstances.
>
> **Second**, we must learn to quiet our inner being, all the voices and thoughts within us that are calling for our attention. Until they are quieted, we most likely will not hear His voice.[9]

The Two Great Hindrances

In our quest for intimacy with God, then, we face two primary hindrances: external distractions and internal chaos. The first involves disturbances and interruptions that come from our surroundings, while the second relates to struggles on the battlefield of our minds. Neither of these will go away on their own or by accident. We must conquer them by firm commitment and deliberate action.

I have found that we need to be free of external distractions so that we can "center down into our hearts." The phrase "center down" in church history comes to us from the Quakers. "Centering" is a truth the Quakers have stewarded for generations, and it is a major part of their theology. Basically, to center down means to recognize the center of quiet in the midst of the storm in our soul—kind of like the eye of a hurricane—and to focus on that center until the surrounding turmoil fades away. Even though our souls may be rushing and roiling, there is a quiet place in the center where God commands peace, and where His Kingdom is manifested.

It is in that center of quiet where we meet God in genuine fellowship and close communion. Achieving quietness of spirit is the means to that end; it is not an end in itself. Again, let me turn to my friends, the Virklers:

> Stillness is not a goal in itself. I want to become still in mind and body so my heart can know and sense God moving within. His promptings are gentle, and until my own inner and outer ragings are quieted, I will not sense His inner moving.
>
> In becoming still, I am not trying to **do anything**. I simply want to be **in touch** with the Divine Lover. I am centered on **this moment** of time and experiencing Him in it.
>
> Becoming still cannot be hurried or forced. Rather, it must be allowed to happen. At a point in your stillness, God takes over and you sense His active flow within you. His spontaneous images begin to flow with life of their own. His voice begins speaking, giving you wisdom and strength. You find that you are "in the Spirit" (Rev. 1:10).[10]

For most of us this center of quiet is not easy to find. Although quietness before God "cannot be hurried or forced," and "must be allowed to happen," it will not come automatically. We must consciously desire it, deliberately plan for it, and diligently pursue it. The rewards of success will justify all the time, energy, effort, and rigorous self-discipline required to get there. We will be at peace in the presence of our Lord.

David summed it up well when he wrote, "Rest in the Lord; wait patiently for Him to act...Don't fret and worry... But all who humble themselves before the Lord shall be given every blessing and shall have wonderful peace."[11]

This type of contemplative waiting on God is just one of many legitimate expressions of prayer. And while it is not a "quick fix" to all of our problems, it is a powerful yet sorely neglected weapon in God's arsenal to help us find His safe path through the perplexing maze of life.

Meditating on Scripture—a Tool of Quieting Oneself

One practice that is very helpful in learning to quiet ourselves before the Lord is to meditate on a passage of Scripture. Understand me here. I'm not talking about some Far East or New Age method of emptying the mind, but rather a focused concentration on a portion of God's Word. We are not to be empty-headed, but rather Christ-minded. As we let our minds dwell on Scripture, the Holy Spirit, who inspired all Scripture, interprets it in our hearts and brings our spirit into harmony with Him. God's Word is alive and active, and meditating on it can usher us into the realm of the Spirit.

Madame Jeanne Guyon (1648-1717) gives us a wise perspective on this idea. A French Christian mystic, Madame Guyon spent much of her life in prison because of her religious beliefs. Even today her devotional writings compel readers to move into a living experience of Jesus Christ. One of her most widely read books is *Experiencing the Depths of the Lord Jesus Christ*, which greatly influenced Watchman Nee, John Wesley, Hudson Taylor, and many others.

> In "beholding the Lord," you come to know the Lord in a totally different way. Perhaps at this point I need to share with you the greatest difficulty you will have in waiting upon the Lord. It has to do with your mind. The mind has a very strong tendency to stray away from the Lord. Therefore, as you come before the Lord to sit in His presence...beholding Him, make use of the Scripture to quiet your mind.
>
> The way to do this is really quite simple. First, read a passage of Scripture. Once you sense the Lord's presence, the content of what you have read is no longer important. The Scripture has served its purpose: it has quieted your mind and brought you to Him.[12]

Meditating on Scripture is different from simply reading it. In meditation, we focus on one or two verses at most, sometimes only part of a verse, a single phrase, or even just one or two words. We mull over those words, chewing on them, reflecting on them, and turning them over in our minds to look at them from every angle. As we concentrate on the Scripture, the Holy Spirit will use the living Word of God to bring us into the presence of God Himself. (More on the subject of Christian meditative prayer will be brought forth in Chapter Seven.)

Madame Guyon's main point here is that the primary purpose of meditating on Scripture is to bring us to our Beloved. Many times we tend to be too mechanical or too technical in our approach to the Bible. We focus on studying the Scriptures, dissecting and analyzing the verses, formulating theology and doctrine, and such. All that is fine and good, but if we stop there, we miss the point. In fact, we will miss the Person! We don't want to be like the religious leaders, to whom Jesus said, "You search the Scriptures because you think that in them you have eternal life; it is these that testify about Me; and you are unwilling to come to Me so that you may have life."[13] Bible study is very important for us as Christians, but in the end it accomplishes little if it does not lead us into a *personal encounter* with the Divine Author. Remember, we want less of us and more of Him!

We Must Be Ready to Deal With Distractions

Anyone who has ever made a serious attempt to develop an active, consistent prayer life has wrestled with the problem of distractions, both external and internal. It's amazing how, no sooner than we get alone in a quiet place for prayer, interruptions or family "crises" of all sorts occur. Stray thoughts by the score pop up, many of them from way out in left field: *Where in the world did **that** one come from?* There we are, trying to focus on God, and our minds or our circumstances are constantly working to pull our attention away. Many Christians become so discouraged by their repeated failures to enter into focused prayer that they give up completely, in their minds abandoning all hope of getting close to God. From my experience, these thoughts do not hit me when I read a newspaper or magazine. But they sure crop up when I go to read God's Word! Sounds like something or someone (the devil) feels threatened!

But if we are serious about being intimate with the Lord, we will have to deal with the problem of distractions. In this regard, Madame Guyon gives us some wise counsel.

> What about distractions? Let's say your mind begins to wander. Once you have been deeply touched by the Lord's Spirit and are distracted, be diligent to bring your wandering

mind back to the Lord. This is the easiest way in the world to overcome external distractions....

When your mind has wandered, don't try to deal with it by changing what you are thinking. You see, if you pay attention to what you are thinking, you will only irritate your mind and stir it up more! Instead, withdraw from your mind! Keep turning within to the Lord's presence. By doing this, you will win the war with your wandering mind and yet never directly engage in the battle...

As you begin this venture you will, of course, discover that it is difficult to bring your mind under control. Why is this? Because through many years of habit, your mind has acquired the ability to wander all over the world, just as it pleases, so what I speak of here is something that is to serve as a discipline to your mind....

Be assured that as your soul becomes more accustomed to withdrawing to inward things, this process will become easier. There are two reasons you will find it easier each time to bring your mind under subjection to the Lord: first of all, the mind—after much practice—will form a new habit of turning deep within; secondly, you have a gracious Lord![14]

Many of us were taught to deal with stray thoughts during prayer by rebuking them in the name of Jesus. This is a valid and effective strategy, but it has a down side. Once we deal with one wayward thought, another may pop up to take its place, then another, and another. Before we know it we are spending all our time rebuking our thoughts. Madame Guyon says, in effect, that we can win this war not by focusing our attention on the devil, but by *focusing on Jesus*. This doesn't mean we ignore the devil. We deal with the devil by focusing on Jesus, because Jesus is the answer and the antidote to the devil. Focusing on Jesus defeats the devil because it helps us to ignore distractions and to "center down" on the Lord's holy Presence.

Sometimes We Use Outer Distractions to Run From Inner Turmoil

We can minimize external distractions by finding a quiet time and place to seek the Lord's presence away from telephones, TVs, computers, and other trappings of modern life. Unfortunately, this often is not enough. Once we have silenced the outer voices, we still have to contend with the restlessness of our minds. If anything will reveal to us just how chaotic and undisciplined our minds can be, it is when we try to develop the habit of solitude.

Henri Nouwen (1932-1996), a Catholic priest and psychologist, offers some helpful insights on the matter. Born in Holland, Nouwen came to the United States in 1964. During his life he taught at numerous universities and authored several books, including *Making All Things New*, from which the following is taken.

> To bring some solitude into our lives is one of the most necessary but also most difficult disciplines. Even though we may have a deep desire for real solitude, we also experience a certain apprehension as we approach that solitary place and time. As soon as we are alone, without people to talk with, a book to read, TV to watch, or phone calls to make, an inner chaos opens up in us.
>
> This chaos can be so disturbing and so confusing that we can hardly wait to get busy again. Entering a private room and shutting the door, therefore, does not mean that we immediately shut out all of our inner doubts, anxieties, fears, bad memories, unresolved conflicts, angry feelings and impulsive desires. On the contrary, when we have removed our outer distractions, we often find that our outer distractions manifest themselves to us in full force.
>
> We often use these outer distractions to shield ourselves from interior noises. It is thus not surprising that we have a difficult time being alone. The confrontation with our inner conflicts can be too painful for us to endure.
>
> This makes the discipline of solitude all the more important! Solitude is not a spontaneous response to an occupied and preoccupied life. There are too many reasons not to be alone. Therefore, we must begin by carefully planning some solitude.[15]

The first time I read this, I was so relieved to find someone else echoing my own experience! I wasn't alone! If the truth be told, most of you could probably say the same thing. We don't find it easy to be alone and quiet because when we are, our minds start racing and all sorts of thoughts, pressed down or suppressed by the busyness of life, clamor their way to the surface. For all these reasons and more, solitude does not come naturally for most of us. If we want it we must, as Nouwen says, plan carefully and deliberately for it.

At First, It May Seem Like a Waste of Time

With this in mind, we shouldn't be discouraged if we don't reach complete quietness of spirit the first time we try. Again, Henri Nouwen:

> Once we have committed ourselves to spending time in solitude, we develop an attentiveness to God's voice in us. In the beginning, during the first days, weeks, or even months, we may have the feeling that we are simply wasting our time. Time in "quietness" may at first seem a little more than a time in which we are bombarded by thousands of thoughts and feelings that emerge from hidden areas of our minds.
>
> One of the early Christian writers describes the first stages of solitary prayer as the experience of a man who, after many years of living with open doors, suddenly decides to shut them. The visitors who used to come and enter start pounding on his doors, wondering why they are not allowed to enter. Only when they realize that they are not welcome do they stop gradually coming.
>
> This is the experience of anyone who decides to enter into solitude after a life without much spiritual discipline. At first, the many distractions keep presenting themselves. Later, as they receive less and less attention, they slowly withdraw.
>
> The discipline of solitude allows us to come in touch with this hopeful presence of God in our lives and allows us to also taste, even now, the beginnings of joy and peace which belong to the new heaven and the new earth.
>
> The discipline of solitude, as I have described it here, is one of the most powerful disciplines in developing a prayer life. It is a simple, though not easy, way to free us from the slavery of our occupations and preoccupations, and to begin to hear that voice that makes all things new.[16]

Stray and unbidden thoughts can arise from any number of different directions. Our minds suddenly fill up with thoughts of things we need to do, people we need to see, phone calls we need to make, unfinished tasks that are hanging over us, etc. Sometimes these thoughts are intrusions from outside our "quiet place." Sometimes they come from the enemy, trying to disrupt our communion. Sometimes God Himself is trying to get our attention.

What Are We to Do?

Whatever the source of these thoughts, how do we deal with them? Let's turn again to *Communion With God* for some very practical counsel regarding the problem of how to remove the inner noise of voices, thoughts, and pressures.

- *Thoughts of things to do.* Write them down so you don't forget them.

- *Thoughts of sin-consciousness.* Confess your sin and clothe yourself with the robe of righteousness.

- *Mind flitting about.* Focus on a vision of Jesus with you.

- *Need to get in touch with your heart.* Begin singing and listening to the spontaneous song bubbling up from your heart.

- *Need for additional time to commune when your mind is poised and still.* Realize that times when you are doing automatic activities (i.e., driving, bathing, exercising, routine jobs, etc.) are ideal times for hearing from God.[17]

At this point, what's important is not where you are presently in your Christian walk but that you are committed to moving forward from where you are toward greater maturity and deeper intimacy. Don't get discouraged if some other Christians you know seem to be farther along than you are. We should never compare our spiritual life to that of any other person. That's a ploy the devil can use to drag us down. Jesus Christ alone is our standard. He will not berate us or belittle us, but love us and patiently lead us into the deeper life of close communion with Him. The Holy Spirit will help us get in touch with the God-life that is within us.

Never for a moment allow yourself to become convinced that waiting on God is a waste of time. *Waiting on God is not time wasted, it is time gained.* Waiting on God is a wise and profitable investment that, in time, will reap abundant dividends in your life.

Sometimes We Have to Take a More Aggressive Approach

I have learned through my own experience that the passive approach to quietness before God is not always enough. The human mind can be a stubborn beast that will not submit without a fight. Sometimes more aggressive measures are needed.

When I was growing up, I was a very good student in school, partly because I taught myself academic disciplines. One of these was the practice of recording my class notes on a reel-to-reel tape recorder (this was before the days of cassettes!) and listening to them as I went to sleep at night. As a result, I knew my notes thoroughly and did very well in class. Another result of this practice was that I developed a "tape recorder brain." I had excellent recall of everything I heard, not only in school, but also anywhere else: conversations, TV shows, movies, etc. Anything audible I could remember in great detail and with great accuracy. In many ways this ability was an asset for me through the years.

There was a down side, however. One consequence of my "tape recorder brain" was that my mind was always active and working. I couldn't shut it down. It seemed as though my mental tape recorder had no "off" button. At night I would lie awake for hours, repeatedly replaying and analyzing conversations and other dialogue from earlier in the day. I did not know how to quiet my mind or calm my spirit. This characteristic of my mental makeup caused me great difficulty when I began seeking to enter into the place of quiet, contemplative prayer and deep communion with the Lord. It was a great struggle for me; I simply did not know how to do it. One of the enemies of communion with God is a mind busy with other things. It's hard to hear the voice of God when you're constantly hearing your own thoughts.

Eventually, over a long period of time and by the grace and power of God, I learned how to bring my mind under submission and how to wait quietly before Him. In the process, I also learned that sometimes we need to take the offensive, aggressively engaging in the battle to control our minds.

One of the favorite Scripture passages for intercessors and other believers engaged in spiritual warfare comes from Paul's second letter to the Corinthians:

> For the weapons of our warfare are not of the flesh, but divinely powerful for the destruction of fortresses. We are destroying speculations and every lofty thing raised up against the knowledge of God, and we are taking every thought captive to the obedience of Christ.[18]

While it is popular to teach these verses in the context of waging war against spiritual principalities and powers, I learned years ago to apply them in the war against the strongholds of my mind. In my own experience, these verses comprise first of all the principle of bringing every thought and activity of the mind under submission to Christ. I began to apply the spiritual weapons of the name and the blood of Jesus against the strongholds of my own thinking, and began to pull them down. I had to learn how to do this before I could apply the contemplative lessons and principles of quietness that Madame Guyon and Henri Nouwen describe.

We Have to Take the Initiative

When I read Second Corinthians 10:4-5, I envision this "battle-field of the mind" in a specific way. These strongholds or "fortress-es" (vs. 4) refer to the ancient wall around our minds. They represent our overall mental attitude, particularly negative and defeatist mind-sets that drag us down. The arguments or "speculations" (vs. 5) are the guards on the wall of human reasoning, while the high or "lofty" things, (vs. 5) are the high towers on the wall of human pride. Final-ly, the "thoughts" (vs. 5) are individual soldiers armed with the weapon of the power of suggestion.

These adversaries will not surrender without a fight. We have to take the initiative, go on the offensive, and "storm the gates" of our mental strongholds. Using the "battering rams" of the name of Jesus, the blood of Jesus (see Rev. 12:11), and God's written and spoken Word (see Mt. 4:3-10), we can prevail and bring every thought "cap-tive to the obedience of Christ."

I'm not saying that it's easy; it isn't. But I will say that with patience, persistence, discipline, and the power of the Spirit we can, over time, tear up the foundations of our old patterns of thinking and lay down new foundations for the new thought patterns and mental attitudes that we develop as new creations in Christ. I believe that this is what the apostle Paul had in mind when he wrote, "Be trans-formed by the renewing of your mind."[19] and "Lay aside the old self...be renewed in the spirit of your mind, and put on the new self, which in the likeness of God has been created in righteousness and holiness of the truth."[20]

Practical Steps to Having the Mind of Christ

In the 4th chapter of Philippians Paul tells us, "Finally, brethren, whatever is true, whatever is honorable, whatever is right, whatever is pure, whatever is lovely, whatever is of good repute, if there is any excellence and if anything worthy of praise, dwell on these things."[21] This is part of what it means to have the "mind of Christ."[22] Before we can make this a practical reality, however, we must first cleanse our minds. This does not happen overnight, but as Christians it is part of our destiny.

There are several practical steps to having the mind of Christ.

- *Confessing.* We need to stay up-to-date in confessing our sins. "If we confess our sins, He is faithful and righteous to forgive us our sins and to cleanse us from all unrighteousness."[23]

- *Forgiving.* We have to forgive anyone who has wronged us. "The heart knows its own bitterness, and a stranger does not share its joy."[24] As we go on the "inward journey," old hurts and offenses will rise up and cry out to us. The road to all healing, as well as to the deeper life of intimacy with God, begins with the path of forgiveness.

- *Forgetting.* An important part of good Christian mental health is the art of forgetting. "Forgetting what lies behind and reaching forward to what lies ahead, I press on toward the goal for the prize of the upward call of God in Christ Jesus."[25] Forgetting does not mean that we develop spiritual amnesia and no longer remember the pain and hurt of the past. It does mean that through the grace of God the debilitating sting of pain is removed so that we can continue the journey.

- *Removing.* There are worldly attitudes, habits, and practices that we need to remove from our lives so that we can focus exclusively on Jesus. "Let us...lay aside every encumbrance and the sin which so easily entangles us, and let us run with endurance the race that is set before us, fixing our eyes on Jesus..."[26]

- *Combating and withstanding.* Sometimes we have to fight before we can obtain an inner peace and serenity. "For the weapons of our warfare are not of the flesh, but divinely powerful for the destruction of fortresses. We are destroying speculations and every lofty thing raised up against the knowledge of God, and we are taking every thought captive to the obedience of Christ."[27]

- *Building up.* Whenever we tear down the negative, we need to build up the positive in its place. "But you, beloved, building yourselves up on your most holy faith, praying in the Holy Spirit, keep yourselves in the love of God, waiting anxiously for the mercy of our Lord Jesus Christ to eternal life."[28] Praying in the Spirit with the gift of tongues has been a great and vital key for me through the years. It is not just a spiritual discipline for me, but a way of life.

- *Putting on.* We have to "dress up" in the new spiritual garments Christ has given us. "Put on the Lord Jesus Christ..."[29] "Put on the full armor of God..."[30] "So, as those who have been chosen of God, holy and beloved, put on a heart of compassion, kindness, humility, gentleness and patience...Beyond all these things put on love, which is the perfect bond of unity."[31]

The Rewards Are Worth the Effort

In the final analysis, where is all of this leading? What are we trying to accomplish by getting quiet and still before God? We are after nothing less than intimate communion with our loving Father, union with Christ, and harmony of our spirit with His Spirit. It is a communion of perfect and abiding love.

Jean Nicholas Grou (1730-1803), a Jesuit priest who lived in Holland and France, entered into a deeper life with God on a retreat in 1767 where he learned to live his life in the spirit of prayer and complete abandonment to God's will. In his classic book *How To Pray*, he gives a beautiful description of this intimate communion.

You ask me what this voice of the heart is. It is love which is the voice of the heart. Love God and you will always be speaking to Him. The seed of love is growth in prayer. If you do not understand that, you have never yet either loved or prayed. Ask God to open your heart and kindle in it a spark of His love and then you will begin to understand what praying means.

If it is the heart that prays, it is evident that sometimes, and even continuously, it can pray by itself without any help from words, spoken or conceived. Here is something which few people understand and which some even entirely deny. They insist that there must be definite and formal acts. They are mistaken, and God has not yet taught them how the heart prays. It is true that the thoughts are formed in the mind before they are clothed in words. The proof of this is that we often search for the right word and reject one after another until we find the right one which expresses our thoughts accurately. We need words to make ourselves intelligible to other people but not to the Spirit. It is the same with the feelings of the heart. The heart conceives feelings and adopts them without any need of resorting to words, unless it wishes to communicate them to others or to make them clear to itself.

For God reads the secrets of the heart. God reads its most intimate feelings, even those which we are not aware of. It is not necessary to make use of formal acts to make ourselves heard by God. If we do make use of them in prayer, it is not so much for God's sake as our own, in that they keep our attention fixed in His presence.

Imagine a soul so closely united to God that it has no need for outward acts to remain attentive to the inward prayer. In these moments of silence and peace, when it pays no heed to what is happening within itself, it prays and prays excellently with a simple and direct prayer that God will understand perfectly by the action of grace. The heart will be full of aspirations towards God without any clear expression. Though they may elude our own consciousness, they will not escape the consciousness of God.

This prayer, so empty of all images and perceptions... apparently so passive and yet so active, is—as far as the limitations of this life allow—pure adoration in spirit and in truth. It is adoration fully worthy of God in which the soul is united to Him as its ground, the created intelligence to the uncreated, without anything but very simple attention of the mind and as equally simple application of the will. This is what is called the prayer of silence, or quiet, or of bare faith.[32]

In Tune With God

That's intimacy with God—to be so in tune with Him that no outward words or actions are necessary, only "pure adoration in spirit and in truth," from our spirit to His Spirit.

Another name for this kind of communion is *contemplative prayer*. Because of some *superficial* similarities it bears to certain occultic and New Age practices, it is extremely important that we have a crystal clear understanding of what contemplative prayer is—and what it is *not*. We will deal with that in the next chapter. At this point, let me say that contemplative prayer is the kind of prayer Jesus had in mind when He said, "But you, when you pray, go into your inner room, close your door and pray to your Father who is in secret, and your Father who sees what is done in secret will reward you."[33]

Hey, remember, time with God is not time wasted, but time gained! Don't you want to walk farther down the road to intimacy and reach deeper into His heart—after all, He is the Lover of our soul!

Father, lead us into these forgotten ways. Silence the inner ragings of voices contending for our attention. Quiet our souls that we may know You and Your precious Son, Jesus. Holy Spirit, take Your liberty to write these laws on our hearts. Lord, we want to know You! Teach us for Your Kingdom's sake. Amen!

Reflection Questions

1. What can be obstacles to greater intimacy with God?
2. In your life, what are the hindrances to greater intimacy with God?
3. What does true communion with God require?

Recommended Reading

Passion for Jesus by Mike Bickle (Creation House, 1993)
The God Chasers by Tommy Tenney (Destiny Image, 1998)
Intimate Friendship With God by Joy Dawson (Chosen, 1986)

Endnotes

1. Lk. 22:19b, 20b.
2. Jn. 13:23.
3. Jn. 19:26; 20:2; 21:7, 20.
4. 1 Jn. 1:1, 3.
5. Ps. 62:1a.
6. Hab. 2:20.
7. 1 Kings 19:12b KJV.
8. Ps. 46:10 KJV.
9. Mark and Patti Virkler, *Communion With God*, Shippensburg, PA: Destiny Image Publishers, Inc., 1990, p. 47.
10. Virkler, p. 48.
11. Ps. 37:7a, 8b, 11 TLB.
12. Jeanne Guyon, *Experiencing God Through Prayer*, Donna C. Arthur, ed., Springdale, PA: Whitaker House, 1984, pp. 9-10.
13. Jn. 5:39-40.
14. Guyon, *Experiencing God Through Prayer*, pp. 11-13.
15. Henri J.M. Nouwen, *Making All Things New*, New York, NY: Ballantine Books, 1983, pp. 69-71.
16. *Ibid*, pp. 73-75.
17. Virkler, *Communion With God*, p. 49.
18. 2 Cor. 10:4-5.
19. Rom. 12:2b.
20. Eph. 4:22b-24.
21. Phil. 4:8.
22. 1 Cor. 2:16b.
23. 1 Jn. 1:9.
24. Prov. 14:10.
25. Phil. 3:13-14.
26. Heb. 12:1b-2a.
27. 2 Cor. 10:4-5.
28. Jude 20-21.
29. Rom. 13:14a.

30. Eph. 6:11a.
31. Col. 3:12, 14.
32. Jean Nicholas Grou, *How to Pray*. As taken from *Devotional Classics*, edited by Richard Foster and James Smith, San Francisco, CA; Harper Collins, 1989, p. 95.
33. Mt. 6:6.

Chapter Three

Understanding Contemplative Prayer

Are you ready to continue on our journey together? My goal is to whet your appetite so much that even the terms "spiritual disciplines" and "devotions" won't sound mundane and boring, but will be revitalized into the real life that they actually are. But you must meet some requirements in order to proceed farther into His presence and truly waste your life on Jesus.

A Heart Like Lydia's

Mary of Bethany gave her tears, her hair, her all. John, the beloved disciple of Jesus, laid his head on the chest of Jesus. What did Lydia of Thyatira do?

> *A woman named Lydia, from the city of Thyatira, a seller of purple fabrics, a worshiper of God, was listening; and the Lord opened her heart to respond to the things spoken by Paul. And when she and her household had been baptized, she urged us, saying, "If you have judged me to be faithful to the Lord, come into my house and stay." And she prevailed upon us.*[1]

Lydia met Paul at the riverside where Jewish women regularly gathered to pray. Like Mary of Bethany, Lydia was a "worshiper" and she listened intently to the gospel message. She became the first convert of Paul's European ministry. She too "wasted her life" on her newfound Lord and apparently consecrated her home for house church meetings.

But the quality of Lydia that draws me to her is found in the phrase "and the Lord opened her heart." True contemplatives have what is called an "open heart"—this of course is in contrast to having a "closed heart." If your heart is closed you won't get very far in plunging the "Inner Depths of the Lord Jesus Christ" as Madame Guyon used to term it.

An open heart...Isn't that what you want? Don't you want to emanate those characteristics of Lydia: worshiping, listening, responding, entreating, and giving to her Lord? The starting blocks of understanding contemplative prayer all stem from being vulnerable and transparent—having an "open heart." Before going farther in this text, stop right now and reach out to the Lover of your soul by asking Him to soften your heart and create in you a heart like Lydia's.

Beyond Techniques

More than anything else, contemplative prayer is about intimacy with God. Although in practice it goes far beyond formulas, techniques, and methodologies, at heart it is really quite simple and basic. Contemplative prayer is about our setting apart regular time *specifically* and *exclusively* for meeting the Lord. I'm talking about much more than a daily "quiet time" with its five minute Scripture and devotional reading and "quickie" prayer (although that's a good place to start, especially if at present you're not getting *any* time alone with God). Contemplative prayer takes time, patience, discipline, and careful cultivation, not because God is elusive or distant, but because *we* have so many negative and unhealthy mental habits to unlearn.

Many Christians today, although desperately hungry for intimacy with God, get nervous at the mention of words like *contemplation, meditation, centering,* and *quietness,* (not to mention the ugly word *discipline!*) because of their modern association with the occult, Eastern mysticism, and New Age. In their minds, these words conjure up images of crystals, channeling, spirit guides, and bare-chested yogis sitting in lotus position while "contemplating" their navels and humming. For this reason, many believers shy away from any involvement in the contemplative aspects of faith.

This is unfortunate because all of these words relate to practices which, used rightly, are thoroughly biblical and are time-honored methods of drawing near to God. The problem is that for centuries the mainstream of the Christian Church has ignored and neglected them until they are virtually a lost art among believers today. As a consequence, the contemplative arts by and large have been appropriated by "counterfeit" groups and movements who falsely promise enlightenment and fulfillment for people who are searching for a more "personal" spirituality than they have found in the traditional church.

But let's make sure our anchor is dropped through the sea of uncertainty and confusion and our boat is grounded well so we won't be toppled over by just any wave that comes crashing in. For a moment, let's take a quick glance at the age old definitions of some of these important terms from Webster's Dictionary:

- **Contemplate** — 1) to gaze at intensely, 2) to think about intensely; to study, 3) to expect or intend; to meditate; muse.

- **Muse** — to think or consider deeply; meditate.

- **Meditate** — to plan; intend; to think deeply; reflect.

- **Reflect** — 1) to throw back (light, heat, or sound), 2) to give back an image (or) mirror, 3) to bring or come back as a consequence; as reflected glory.

- **Reflect on** (or upon) — 1) to contemplate; ponder, 2) to cast blame or discredit.

- **Reflective** — 1) reflecting, 2) of or produced by reflection, 3) meditative; thoughtful.[2]

With this in mind, it is important that we clearly distinguish between biblical contemplative prayer and its pagan, worldly, and demonic counterfeits. Once we understand what contemplative prayer is *not*, we can then delve deeply into what it *is*, as well as discover the benefits it can bring into our lives.

Contemplative Prayer Is Not Eastern Meditation or Mysticism

How do we distinguish Christian contemplative prayer from the world's counterfeits? To start with, Christian contemplative prayer is not a "technique." Neither is it a relaxation therapy exercise, or a form of self-hypnosis or mesmerism. It is not a para-psychological phenomenon. Christian contemplative prayer is not a New Age approach to self-improvement, or an attempt to blank our minds and empty our heads. It is neither a "new thing," nor a makeover of Eastern meditation.

Despite *superficial* appearances of similarity, there are significant differences between Christian contemplative prayer and Eastern meditation.[3]

1. Eastern methods are primarily concerned with "awareness." Contemplative prayer is concerned with divine love between God and a person.

2. Eastern traditions put the greater emphasis upon what self can do. Christian tradition recognizes that our unique individuality was created by God and for God as a vehicle for His expression in the world.

3. Eastern methods seek to get in touch with man's spiritual nature by concentrating on a mantra or some other method of forced concentration. Contemplative prayer presupposes a personal relationship with God, and encompasses a *voluntary* desire to get in touch with our spiritual nature.

4. Eastern methods focus on what a person can do through focused concentration. Contemplative prayer focuses on surrendering to what *only God can do.*

5. Contemplative prayer is not a relaxation exercise such as breathing techniques or yoga. It is a faith relationship where we open ourselves up to our living, personal, loving, Father-God.

Simply stated, Eastern meditation is man-centered, while Christian contemplative prayer is thoroughly *God-centered*. That makes all the difference in the world.

Contemplative Prayer Is Not "New Age"

Christian contemplative prayer is also vastly different from the New Age movement that has captivated the minds and spirits of so many people in our day. In chapter six of their book *Communion With God*, the Virklers provide a clear and thorough discussion of the differences between New Testament Christianity and the New Age movement. Here are some of their comments.

The "New Age Movement" appears to be a loosely knit group of individuals who believe that we have entered into a new age called the age of Aquarius. This age has allegedly replaced the age of Pisces, which represents the Christian era (pisces—fish—Christian symbol). The age of Aquarius (water bearer) is characterized by humanism (in a good sense), brotherhood and love. It is to be a golden age.[4]

Part of the appeal of New Age thought and writing is that they espouse positive values such as life, love, creativity, wholeness, community, and sensitivity and respect for the spiritual aspect of human existence—values that resonate with most Christians. Dig below the surface, however, and the differences become very apparent. There are at least nine major distinctions between New Testament Christianity and the New Age movement.[5] Once we understand these distinctions, it becomes clear that Christian contemplative prayer has no relationship whatsoever with New Age thought and practice.

New Testament Christianity	New Age
Who Is God?	
Yahweh, the Personal Creator	The Evocative Other
The Standard of Truth	
The Bible	Evolving, eclectic
Who Is Jesus Christ?	
The Son of God	An enlightened teacher
What About Salvation?	
Purchased by the blood of Jesus	No such thing, or the process of integration
The Focus	
Christ centered	Man centered
The Power	
Through Christ	Through man
The Wisdom	
God's wisdom	Man's wisdom
The Next Age	
Brought about by God	Brought about by man
The Stance	
Man receiving from God	Man reaching to become god

One reason the New Age is so deceptive is that it espouses ideals and values that are very similar to Christianity. This, of course, should be expected, considering the fact that satan is the great counterfeiter...

We recognize that because New Agers are part of the great counterfeit, they may use words, phrases and techniques that have been borrowed from Christianity or Christian traditions. **Yet, we will not give over either these words or these experiences to the satanic counterfeit, as they are God's forever.** For example, New Agers have written on "the rainbow," which of course was part of God's covenant with Noah, and on "centering," which is a word and an experience that has been used for decades by the Quaker church…That does not concern us. We have a standard, the Word of God, and our acceptance of a truth is not based on whether or not a counterfeit group has yet picked it up. We look to see if it is taught in Scripture; and surely such things as centering or quieting our souls before the Lord…is clearly taught and demonstrated by King David in the Psalms as he states "My soul waits in silence for God only (Ps. 62:1, 5)."

Therefore we will expect the New Age to blur the line between truth and error through their eclectic nature, but we will walk calmly according to the eternal truths and experiences taught in God's Word. We shall not concern ourselves with how many cults are also drawing upon biblical concepts. We shall only concern ourselves with encountering fully and completely the God of Scriptures.[6]

It's Time to Reclaim Territory Abandoned to the Enemy

For centuries, the Christian Church has virtually abandoned to the enemy the arena of "spiritual" experiences and supernatural encounters. That is why my wife and I co-authored the book *Encounters With a Supernatural God*. It's time for the Church to rise up and reclaim that territory. Read through the following and see if you do not agree:

One thing the New Age calls Christians to do is to enter fully into all of the dimensions of our relationship with Christ. The New Age has arisen to take the territory abandoned by the mainstream Christianity. Because Christianity (even most Charismatics) has neglected the intuitive and relational and has majored on the propositional and the analytical, a void has been left in the hearts of those who were seeking spiritual encounters…The very best antidote for the New Age teachings is for Christians to enter into and live fully in the supernatural. This is certainly no time to draw back from supernatural living and retreat into a mere defense of orthodoxy…Since the dawn of history, when God's people do not preach, proclaim and model the genuine article, men and women will wander into whatever appears to offer the fulfillment of their spiritual quest. We need to cast aside our hesitation and proceed strongly forward, the Word and the Spirit as our unfailing guide…

Therefore, I believe the New Age is satan's reaction to the mighty outpouring of the Holy Spirit that we are seeing in this century. I do not see it as something to fear or to flee from. Since when does light fear darkness? No, I stand against it in the power of the Holy Spirit, and in the power of Almighty God![7]

We Must "Test the spirits," and Then Proceed With Faith

It's time that we in the Church got over our fear of being deceived. Many of us have been reluctant to enter into the inward life for fear of tapping into the wrong kind of spirit, or of proceeding in an unbiblical manner. The fact is, the enemy counterfeits only things that are *genuine* and *authentic*. We can no longer afford to sit idly by while satan lures and deceives the world with his cheap, false imitations of the precious truths of God. With holy boldness and Spirit-power we must stand and reclaim the land of meditation, contemplation, quietness, revelation, ecstasy, visions, and angelic encounters for His name's sake!

Of course, we need to "test the spirits" and confirm every teaching, belief, and practice by the Bible and by the witness of truly godly leadership. At the same time, we need to remember that satan always tries to inject fear into the Church, and where that wrong kind of fear is concerned, "perfect love casts out fear."[8] We must never allow a "spirit of fear" sent by the enemy to enslave our hearts just because it sometimes sneaks into the Church under the guise of "appropriate caution" and "respectability." We must proceed in and with faith.

Nevertheless, a few prudent cautions are in order as we prepare to pursue the contemplative arts and enter further into the supernatural realm.

1. Maintain a balance between the inner life and the outward, active life of servanthood. Contemplative prayer is meant to bring an enabling into our life of service.

2. Spiritual consolation from direct contact with God can be so satisfying that it can become a trap. We can seek interior prayer out of a desire to escape rather than out of love. It can become an act of selfish withdrawal rather than self-surrender.

3 The beauty of contemplative prayer is so incomparable, its effect so affirming, and its power so transforming

that it can lead to spiritual gluttony. Beware of seeking only consolation instead of seeking God Himself.

4. Use common sense and don't overdo it. We need to jealously guard the purity of our intentions. Remember, we are to advance—not retreat!

How Do You Describe the Indescribable?

So then, what *is* contemplative prayer? It's very hard to adequately describe it in words because it is experiential. Any of you who have ever had a deeply moving emotional or spiritual experience know how difficult it is to explain it to someone else.

In 1991 I had a dream in which the Holy Spirit said to me, "I will reveal the hidden streams of the prophetic to you." For a long time I thought this meant that He would bring me into contact with different prophetic people around the world of whom I was unaware. I have since come to understand that the primary meaning of my dream was that the Lord would lead me into the world of the "desert fathers" and the Christian "mystics" of times past. These were contemplatives who pursued the daily presence of God, and of whom little or nothing has been known by the vast majority of Christians today, particularly those of us in the Protestant evangelical and charismatic wing of the church.

Shortly after I had this dream I embarked on a yearlong adventure during which I read nothing but Catholic and Orthodox literature. I think I drove my wife about crazy. She began to wonder if I had really gone over the edge. I was simply trying to gain some understanding of the principles of contemplative prayer and the quiet life before God. In the process I discovered writings and teachings that have since become my lifelong friends. Today, my wife and I both appreciate and glean from the writings of many of these devotional mystics.

In October 1994, the Holy Spirit gave me another installment through a word in which He said, "I will teach you to release the highest weapon of spiritual warfare—the brilliance of My great presence." The highest weapon of spiritual warfare is *God Himself*! I believe that there is a place where we can pick up the dew of God, the very essence of His person. The journey to that place is down a road less traveled, a road strewn with the bodies of martyrs and other saints who were excommunicated or subjected to other forms of church "discipline" simply because they sought deep personal communion with God. It is a path filled with people whose hearts have been captured by the Lord Jesus Christ; people who have given themselves to become very heavenly minded, in order that they might become of great earthly good. Sounds like some others before us have been wasted on Jesus as well!

The Problem With Mystical Language

One of the reasons the experiences of mystics and contemplatives have been misunderstood is that they are indescribable. It is one thing to experience the grace of God's intimate nearness; it is another to be able to communicate it. Sometimes someone who truly has a contemplative experience of God expresses it in a way that upsets the more conservative culture of the church and society. Such a person is often labeled a heretic when in reality he is simply expressing himself clumsily.

Mystical language is not doctrinal or theological language. It is the language of the bedchamber, of intimacy, of love; hence, hyperbole and exaggeration abound. If a husband says that he adores his wife, it does not mean that he regards her as an idol or goddess, he is just trying to express his deep feelings of love in a language that is powerless to fully convey them, except by excessive hyperbole. If we begin using such intimate love language in trying to describe our experiences with God, some people may not understand that kind of language, and may think that we are under the influence of "another kind of spirit."

As our contemplative inner experience with God deepens, it may become increasingly difficult to speak about. It may be so precious and so sublime that it becomes as holy to us as it is to God. That is the language of the heart, a language too deep for words. In the end, we are reduced to the simple confession of Walter Hilton: Contemplation is "love on fire with devotion."[9]

Contemplative Prayer Immerses Us Into the Silence of God

Before we delve into any kind of "formal" description of contemplative prayer, let's listen to what some Christian leaders through the years have to say from their own experience. In his outstanding book *Prayer: Finding The Heart's True Home*, Richard Foster, a contemporary author and teacher, writes:

> Contemplative Prayer immerses us into the silence of God. How desperately we in the modern world need this wordless baptism! We have become, as the early Church father Clement of Alexandria says, like old shoes—all worn out

except for the tongue...Contemplative prayer is the one discipline that can free us from our addiction to words...

Progress in intimacy with God means progress towards silence...The desert father Ammonas, a disciple of Saint Anthony, writes: I have shown you the power of silence, how thoroughly it heals and how fully pleasing it is to God...Know that it is by silence that the saints grew, that it was because of silence that the power of God dwelt in them, because of silence that the mysteries of God were known to them.[10]

It is this recreating silence to which we are called in contemplative prayer.

Bernard of Clairvaux, a monk and a religious and political leader in 12th century France, gave this description of God's loving attentiveness during contemplation: "We felt that He was present, I remember later that He has been with me; I have sometimes even had a presentiment that He would come; I never felt His coming or leaving."[11]

The Jewel of Contemplative Prayer Has Many Facets

At its core, contemplative prayer is indescribable. However, just as a precious jewel reflects and refracts light in myriad ways as we examine each facet, so we can gain some understanding of contemplative prayer by looking at some "snapshot" descriptions, each of which will help us see it in a slightly different light.[12]

1. *Contemplative prayer is an exercise in letting go of the control of our own life that is produced by leaning on the props of the false self.* The "false self" is the "old self" of Ephesians 4:22. It is the ego-centered self-life that trusts in false things of the world in a search for happiness, fulfillment, peace, purpose, and meaning in life. The false self clings to control out of fear. Contemplative Prayer means letting go of that fear and giving control to God.

2. *Contemplative prayer is a kind of communion intended to increase our intimacy with God and awareness of His presence.*

3. *Contemplative prayer is a step of submission where we place our being at God's disposal and request His work of purification.*

4. *Contemplative prayer is opening ourselves up to the Holy Spirit, to get in touch with our true selves and to facilitate*

an abiding state of union with God. Union with God means being made one with our Master and Creator God. It is a work that God works in our hearts with two vital preparations on our side: love of God and purity of heart.

5. *Contemplative prayer is an exercise in self-surrender. It teaches us to yield, let go, and not be possessive.*

6. *Contemplative prayer is a method of exposing and disengaging from the ordinary obstacles to our awareness of God's presence with us. This prayer is not an end, but a beginning.* It's easy to give in to the temptation to chase after the enemy every time he shows himself; sometimes it's the right thing to do. There is a better way to defeat him— fix our eyes and our hearts steadfastly on Jesus. His light will drive out the darkness.

7. *Contemplative prayer is being still in order to know God (Ps. 46:10).*

8. *Contemplative prayer cultivates our desire to forget ourselves and know God by faith. It is our consent for God's presence and action to take over (Col. 3:10).*

9. *Contemplative prayer is a movement beyond conversation; a discipline to foster that leads us into greater faith, hope, and love.*

10. *Contemplative prayer is an exercise in resting in God. It is not a state of suspension of all activity, but the reductions of many acts to a simple act of saying yes to God's presence during a time of inner, quiet, devotional prayer.*

11. *Contemplative prayer is the trusting and loving faith by which God elevates the human person and purifies the conscious and unconscious obstacles in us that oppose the values of the gospel and the work of the Spirit.*

12. *Contemplative prayer is an activity aimed at fostering the conviction and realization that God lives in us!*

13. *Contemplative prayer is an exercise in purifying our intentions to desire only one thing—God. It is an act of love, a desire not for the experience of God, but for God Himself.*

14. *Contemplative prayer is a discipline that facilitates not only living in God's presence but out of God's presence. Its transforming effects cause the divine Word to once again be incarnated in human form. In other words, it's like God taking on flesh in us.*

15. *Contemplative prayer is a discipline that enables our developing relationship with Jesus Christ to reach stages of growth in union with God.*

Contemplative Prayer Means Hushing All Outward and Earthly Affections

If these "snapshots" of contemplative prayer make the whole thing seem overwhelming to you, remember this: great rewards await those who are willing to pay the price. This is *not* easy; that's why it is called a *discipline*! We will never casually or accidentally enter into an intimate walk with God. Such a walk is reserved for those who deliberately commit and diligently seek it. So don't give up!

We can all take heart from the words of Francois Fenelon, a Quietist leader in France during the late 1600s and early 1700s, who wrote from first-hand experience.

> Be silent, and listen to God. Let your heart be in such a state of preparation that His Spirit may impress upon you such virtues as will please Him. Let all within you listen to Him. This silence of all outward and earthy affection and of human thoughts within us is essential if we are to hear His voice. This listening prayer does indeed involve a hushing of all outward and earthly affection.

> Don't spend your time making plans that are just cobwebs— a breath of wind will come and blow them away. You have withdrawn from God and now you find that God has withdrawn the sense of His presence from you. Return to Him and give Him everything without reservation. There will be no peace otherwise. Let go of all your plans—God will do what He sees best for you.

> Even if you were to alter your plans through earthly means, God would not bless them. Offer Him your tangled mess and He will turn everything toward His own merciful purpose. And the most important thing is to go back to communion with God—even if it seems dry and you are easily distracted.[13]

Contemplative Prayer Is Loving God for His Own Sake

Thomas Merton, a 20th century writer and priest, wrote a book called *Contemplative Prayer*. Even though it was directed primarily to his disciples and students and deals particularly with the monastic lifestyle, Merton's book contains many beautiful gems of wisdom and insight that we can benefit from.

> Without the spirit of contemplation in all our worship—that is to say without the adoration and love of God above all, for his own sake, because he is God—the liturgy will not nourish a really Christian apostolate based on Christ's love and carried out in the power of the *Pneuma* [Spirit].

> The most important need in the Christian world today is this inner truth nourished by this Spirit of contemplation: the praise and love of God, the longing for the coming of Christ, the thirst for the manifestation of God's glory, his truth, his justice, his kingdom in the world. These are all characteristically "contemplative" and eschatological aspirations of the Christian heart, and they are the very essence of monastic prayer. Without them our apostolate is more for our own glory rather than the glory of God...

> Without contemplation and interior prayer the Church cannot fulfill her mission to transform and save mankind. Without contemplation, she will be reduced to being the servant of cynical and worldly powers, no matter how hard her faithful may protest that they are fighting for the Kingdom of God.

> Without true, deep contemplative aspirations, without a total love for God and an uncompromising thirst for his truth, religion tends in the end to become an opiate.[14]

Contemplative Prayer Helps Us Become Aware of the Presence of God

Are the benefits and rewards of contemplative prayer truly worth the disciplined effort and time required to realize them? Don't simply take my word for it. The only way you will ever know for sure is to take the journey yourself. If you need further encouragement, consider the following benefits of contemplative prayer.[15]

1. *By means of contemplative prayer, the Spirit heals the roots of self-centeredness and becomes the source of our conscious activity.*

2. *Contemplative prayer helps us to become aware of the presence of God. Living out of that awareness, we gain strength to meet opposition and contradiction without feeling threatened. The continuing awareness of divine love saves us from*

the need of human affirmation and recognition. It heals negative feelings we have about ourselves.

3. *This form of transforming prayer fosters a different attitude towards one's feelings; it puts them in a different frame of reference. Many of our negative feelings come from a sense of insecurity and the need to build up the empire of self, especially when we feel threatened. But when you are constantly being reaffirmed by God's loving presence, you are no longer afraid to be contradicted or imposed on. Humility will grow as you mature in God's lavish love.*

4. *Contemplative prayer leads us below the conversational level into communion with Him. It basically makes God "more real" to us.*

5. *As our trust in God and our awareness of His love for us increase, we are less afraid to have our dark side exposed. We are enabled to "walk in the light as He...is in the light...the blood of Jesus...cleanses us from all sin."[16] (If the truth be known, God has always known the dark side of our character, has loved us all the time, and is now letting us in on His special secret.)*

6. *The interior silence of contemplative prayer brings such a profound cleansing to our whole being that our emotional blocks begin to soften up and our system begins to flush out these poisonous toxins. Bondages may be broken and strongholds destroyed.*

7. *Although great interior peace may be experienced, this is not the goal. The purpose is not even union with God in a prayer experience. It is to transform us to carry this wholeness with God into the other aspects of everyday life. We are not seeking experiences, but the permanent abiding awareness of being joined to God.*

8. *Contemplative prayer will enable us to walk for and with others with liberty of spirit because we are no longer seeking our own ego-centered goals but responding to reality as it is with His divine love.*

9. *Union with God enables us to handle greater trials. God does not make us like Him just so He can look at us! He wants us to release the fragrance of Christ wherever we go.*

10. *Contemplative prayer teaches us patience, to wait on God, strength for interior silence, and makes us sensitive to the delicate movements of the Spirit in daily life and ministry.*

11. *Contemplative prayer illuminates the source and strengthens the practice of all other types of devotions. It gets us in touch with the divine life dwelling in us, thus aiding all spiritual disciplines in becoming relational practices.*

12. *This divine life is actually going on within us 24 hours a day. Much of the time we do not see it, experience it, or release it. Thus we live out of the false empire of self, shutting down the flow of God's divine presence and love.*

13. *Contemplative prayer aids us in identifying, experiencing, and releasing His life in and through us as we continue to cultivate the wondrous progression of being immersed into His healing love.*

14. *As Madame Guyon stated, "This is why God sends a fire to the earth. It's to destroy all that is impure in you. Nothing can resist the power of that fire. It consumes* every thing. *His Wisdom burns away all the impurities in a man for one purpose:* to leave him fit for divine union."[17]

The Road to Contemplative Prayer
Is a Series of Progressive Steps

While there are no hard and fast rules to go by, generally speaking there is a series of three progressive steps or phases that we will pass through on our way to the region of contemplative prayer. Many of the writers and mystics have identified these progressive steps as recollection, the prayer of quiet, and spiritual ecstasy.

The first phase, recollection, means allowing the Holy Spirit to cast light upon our fragmentation so as to bring cleansing and healing into our souls. It means learning to let go of all competing distractions and focus neither on the past (our guilt, woundedness, etc.) nor on the future (guidance, words, promises of God not yet fulfilled), but on the present—God in the "here and now." Recollection means learning to follow Simon Peter's injunction to cast all our anxiety on Him because He cares for us.[18]

As we begin to rest in the Lord, we should ask the Holy Spirit to make Jesus real to us. We should close everything off and try to picture Jesus sitting in a chair across from us, for He truly is present. God created the human imagination, and utilizing it in contemplation is not only appropriate, but also one of the best uses we can make of it. This is not the same as New Age imaging but simply practicing the presence of God.

If frustration and distractions attempt to press in, we should not follow them. Instead, we should lift them up to the Father, let Him care for them, and allow His "Peace, be still" to silence our noisy hearts. This centeredness does not come easily or quickly, but simply recognizing this fact is a step in the right direction. Another positive stride forward is when we recognize our inability to conquer these distractions in our own strength. That creates in us a necessary sense of dependence on God.

Richard Foster gives a beautiful description of phase two—the prayer of quiet.

> As we grow accustomed to the unifying grace of recollection, we are ushered into a second step in Contemplative Prayer, what Teresa of Avila calls, "The prayer of quiet." We have through recollection put away all obstacles of the heart, all distractions of the mind, all vacillations of the will. Divine graces of love and adoration wash over us like ocean waves. ...At the center of our being we are hushed. ...There is stillness to be sure, but it is a listening stillness. Something deep inside us has been awakened and brought to attention. Our spirit is on tiptoe—alert and listening. There is an inward steady gaze of the heart sometimes called beholding the Lord. We bask in the warmth of his presence...
>
> As we wait before the Lord, graciously we are given a teachable spirit.[19]

The Final Stage

The final step in contemplative prayer is spiritual ecstasy. The word "ecstasy" is derived from the Greek word *ekstasis*, which is often translated in the New Testament as "trance." Spiritual ecstasy is an activity initiated by the Holy Spirit where one is "caught up" into a realm of the Spirit so as to receive those things that God desires (revelations, visions, etc.) It is not an activity that we undertake, but a work that God does upon us. Ecstasy is contemplative prayer taken to the "nth" degree. This step is quite rare. Even the recognized authorities in the contemplative life found it to be a fleeting experience rather than a staple diet.

So what is spiritual ecstasy like? Theodore Brackel, a Dutch Pietist in the 17th century, recorded as best he could his own experience. "I was...transported into such a state of joy and my thoughts were so drawn upward that, seeing God with the eyes of my soul, I felt…God's being and at the same time I was so filled with joy, peace and sweetness, that I cannot express it. With my spirit I was entirely in heaven for two or three days."[20]

In contemplative prayer, our goal should never be to "achieve" spiritual ecstasy, or even to seek any particular kind of experience or spiritual "manifestation." Our sole purpose is simply to *be with God* in that central place of quiet in our spirits, where He is and remains our all in all, and where we live to worship and adore Him, waiting patiently and humbly for His voice, and basking in the warm glow of His eternal love.

Closer to the Presence of the Lord

Teresa of Avila, a 16th century mystic, described this inner journey of the spirit as a progression through seven "mansions," each one leading her closer and closer to the presence of God until finally, in the last one, the Lord Himself was present in glory. She wrote the details of her vision in the classic book *The Interior Castle*. That's where our journey of reaching to the Lover of our soul takes us in the next chapter. It's just another step in pouring your life out as a drink offering for your Lord.

Hey, take His arm and let Him be your escort as He walks you down this ancient pathway less traveled. Lead on, O King Eternal, You have opened our hearts like You opened Lydia's of old.

Reflection Questions

1. What do the words *contemplate* or *contemplative* mean?
2. What is the difference between the New Age practices and Christian Contemplative Prayer?
3. Describe your devotional love relationship with your Lord…do you long to go deeper with Him?

Recommended Reading

Prayer: Finding the Heart's True Home by Richard L. Foster (Harper Collins, 1992)

Communion With God by Mark and Patti Virkler (Destiny Image, 1990)

Contemplative Prayer by Pat Gastineau (Word of Love Ministries, 1999)

Endnotes

1. Acts 16:14-15.
2, Jim W. Goll, *Consecrated Contemplative Prayer*, Antioch, TN: Ministry to the Nations, 1997, p.45.
3. This discussion of the differences between contemplative prayer and Eastern meditation is adapted from a teaching by my friend, Dr. Steve Meeks. Steve is the pastor of the Calvary Community Church, Houston, Texas. He is a Southern Baptist and has a doctorate from the world's largest seminary, in Fort Worth, Texas. Steve is much more advanced in his understanding and experience of the contemplative ways than I am. On numerous occasions he has spent days at a time in monasteries, taking vows of silence and doing research. I appreciate and respect the pilgrimage that Steve is on. His friendship and insights have been an inspiration and an encouragement to me in my own journey.
4. Mark and Patti Virkler, *Communion with God*, Shippensburg, PA: Destiny Image Publishers, Inc., 1990, p. 83.
5. *Ibid.* pp. 83-84.
6. *Ibid.* pp. 84-85.
7. *Ibid.* p. 86.
8. 1 Jn. 4:18b.
9. Walter Hilton, *The Stairway of Perfection*, as quoted in, Richard L. Foster, *Prayer: Finding the Heart's True Home*, New York, NY: Harper San Francisco, a Division of Harper Collins Publishers, 1992, p. 160.
10. Richard L. Foster, *Prayer: Finding the Heart's True Home*, New York, NY: Harper San Francisco, a Division of Harper Collins Publishers, 1992, p. 155.
11. Bernard of Clairvaux, "Sermon LXXXIII on the Song of Songs,"as quoted in Foster, *Prayer: Finding the Heart's True Home*, p. 158.
12. Some of the material in this section was adapted from the teachings of my friend, Dr. Steven Meeks.
13. Francois Fenelon, *The Seeking Heart*, Sargent, GA: Christian Books Publishing House, 1962, p. 88.
14. Thomas Merton, *Contemplative Prayer*, New York, NY: Doubleday, 1996, pp. 115-116.
15. Again, the material in this section was adapted from the teachings of my friend, Dr. Steven Meeks.
16. 1 Jn. 1:7.
17. Madame Jeanne Guyon, *Experiencing the Depths of the Lord Jesus Christ*, as quoted in Foster, pp. 160-161.
18. 1 Pet. 5:7.
19. Richard L. Foster, *Prayer: Finding the Heart's True Home*, p. 163.
20. Theodore Brackel, as quoted in Foster, *Prayer: Finding the Heart's True Home*, p. 164.

Chapter Four

Journey Into the Interior Castle

The inward journey is an excursion deeper and deeper into our souls toward the very center, where God dwells. One of the great "mysteries" of the Christian faith is the truth that the infinite Creator God can abide within the spirits of His greatest creation, His people. This is the mystery that the apostle Paul calls "Christ in you, the hope of glory."[1] How can this be? Believers have pondered and wondered over this for centuries, but no one has ever been able to adequately explain it. It is truly indescribable. The best we can do is simply to attest to the fact that the Bible plainly teaches it, and accept it in faith.

Time after time, Paul returns to this theme in his letters: "For the temple of God is holy, and that is what you are."[2] "Or do you not know that your body is a temple of the Holy Spirit who is in you, whom you have from God, and that you are not your own?"[3] "For we are the temple of the living God; just as God said, 'I will dwell in them and walk among them; and I will be their God, and they shall be My people.' "[4]

The concept of God's people as a living temple for His dwelling was also familiar to the apostle Peter.

> *And coming to Him as to a living stone which has been rejected by men, but is choice and precious in the sight of God, you also, as living stones, are being built up as a spiritual house for a holy priesthood, to offer up spiritual sacrifices acceptable to God through Jesus Christ.*[5]

What these Scriptures tell us is that we are temples of the living God. We are His "house," where He has taken up permanent residence. Just as houses have windows, there are "windows" in our soul. God likes to "wash" our windows, put His face up to them, and look out. That's how visions occur. When God looks through the "windows" of our soul, we catch glimpses of glory because then we see things the way God sees them.

Past the Outer Court

As Christians, we are temples of the living God. Unfortunately, most people and the vast majority of believers spend their entire lives fixing up, painting up, adorning the exterior of the house only. So many are content to stay in the "outer court," never venturing into the deeper rooms and recesses of the temple, or into that Most Holy Place where the Lord Himself dwells in fullness.

It is not God's desire that we remain in the outer court; He wants us to come all the way in so that we can enjoy full fellowship with Him. We can see this in Jesus' words to His disciples the night before He was crucified.

> *Do not let your heart be troubled; believe in God, believe also in Me. In My Father's house are many dwelling places; if it were not so, I would have told you; for I go to prepare a place for you. If I go and prepare a place for you, I will come again and receive you to Myself, that where I am, there you may be also.*[6]

Now certainly, this is a reference to Heaven, and to Jesus' promise to return for us and to take us to be with Him forever. For our immediate purposes, however, I would like to look at these verses from a slightly different angle.

The Innermost Place

Let me begin with a question: *Where* is the Father's house? In Heaven, surely, but according to the verses we have already looked at, God's house is also in *us*. It is us! *We* are His house, His temple! In that house are "many dwelling places," and Jesus has already gone there to "prepare" a place for us. He resides in the fullness of His being in the deepest recesses of our spirit, and is preparing to *receive* us to Himself in that innermost place.

There are many different "rooms" we must pass through on our way to the heart of God's house. In every room we are still in the "Father's house" and under the warm glow of His love and grace, but only in the inmost room will we experience complete communion, oneness of spirit, and the wellsprings of His presence without measure. That's the invitation He extends to us, and the priceless treasure that the inward journey draws us toward.

The Vision of Seven Doors

A few years ago I was in Chicago teaching at a Youth With A Mission school on the subjects of worship, warfare, and intercession. One afternoon a friend of mine and I got off in a room by ourselves and spent some time in quietness, waiting on the Lord together. After awhile I began to receive an interactive vision, and I talked through it quietly with my friend.

In my vision I saw a succession of seven doorways, arranged one after the other as in a tunnel. Each doorway was open, allowing free access to the next one. Words were written on the archway above each door. Above the first doorway were the words, "The Inward Journey." I passed through that doorway and came to the second, which read, "Forgiveness." This was the "room" of the spirit that dealt with freedom from guilt and having a clean and clear conscience.

Passing through the second room, I came to the third doorway, labeled "Cleansed by the Blood." This room moved beyond simple forgiveness to the issue of sanctification. Just because we have been forgiven doesn't necessarily mean that the reality of that forgiveness has penetrated our minds and emotions. We may still struggle for awhile with feelings of guilt or condemnation over our sin. The third room of sanctification dealt with the cleansing of the mind through the power of the blood of Jesus.

As I continued in this visionary experience, written above the fourth doorway were the words, "Lowliness of Heart." This room was all about humility—a true key to the Kingdom of God. When we honestly see Him, the only response we can have is one of humility and lowliness of heart. Humility is one of the keys to the Kingdom. Jesus said, "Blessed are the poor in spirit, for theirs is the kingdom of heaven."[7]

The fifth doorway was marked "Grace." Anything that we receive from Heaven is by the grace of God. There was a time when I would have had to sit down outside the fifth doorway because, even though I knew Jesus and had been forgiven and cleansed, I did not know by revelation what grace was really all about. The Lord had finally given me that understanding, however, so I was able to move through the room of grace.

I Stopped Short of Mercy

Above the sixth doorway was the word "Mercy," with the word "Compassion" underneath it, and it was here, in my vision, that I had to stop. I looked through the sixth doorway to the seventh, and saw that it was marked, "Union with Christ." How I ached and longed to go through the seventh doorway into greater union with Christ! I had come so far, but now I was stalled at the doorway of mercy. Just as I had needed a revelation of grace to pass through that room, I needed a revelation of mercy—to understand it and have it brought into my life—in order to pass through the doorway into the sixth room.

It was not so much a revelation of God's mercy to me that I needed, but that I was to extend mercy to others in the name and Spirit of Christ. Once we receive a revelation of mercy, we begin to exhibit the God-life that is within us, and to release that God-life to others in mercy and compassion. That's where I was hung up.

Six is the number of man. At the time I received this vision, I had just come through a very difficult time of controversy and upheaval in my life and was still struggling with a lot of emotional pain and spiritual disappointment. A man I greatly admired and respected, who was a prophetic tutor to me and had greatly impacted my life, had fallen into some major difficulties and pressures which resulted with him being temporarily removed from the ministry. As a younger man in the ministry myself, I was disappointed, disillusioned, angry, and deeply hurt.

That anger, deeper than anything I had ever experienced before, began to spill over into many of my closest relationships. I had never known that such anger existed inside me. I didn't want it, but there it was. Instead of extending mercy as Christ did, I wanted to throw stones. I was torn between taking a stand for righteousness and the need at the same time to be compassionate and caring. All I knew was that I felt ripped off and my internal emotional state showed it.

In my vision I realized that until I could deal with the mercy issue in my heart, I would not be able to progress through the seventh doorway into greater union with Christ. I longed desperately for that union, but I knew that I had not yet come to the place of understanding the great mercy and compassion that God has toward all of us. I knew I had a long way to go. At times I felt hopeless—even a prisoner to other judgments concerning me.

The Lord Said, "The Door of Mercy Is Open."

So I embarked on a journey to get mercy worked into my life. I began reading about mercy and asking God for revelations of mercy. Whenever we are wounded or hurt or disappointed, the natural thing we want to do is hide. I prayed to the Lord to change me in my innermost place, and to help me stop hiding behind all the defensive barriers I had put up. I needed to be willing to make myself vulnerable again.

One morning a few years later, the Holy Spirit spoke to my heart about times of refreshing that He was going to bring to the Body of Christ across the nations. He spoke to me of several different things, but the very last thing He said to me was very personal. He said, "The door of mercy is open; step in." How my heart leapt and my spirit rejoiced when I heard those words! I sighed deeply and by faith stepped into a new room filled with new understandings and ways of God.

Stepping Through the Doorway

Through the grace and mercy of God, I have since been reconciled on the personal side with this prophetic minister whose fall so deeply hurt me. Much of our original relationship has been restored. In the process I have learned a lot about the mercy of God. Being able to *receive* mercy is only part of the picture. It's only when we learn to *give* mercy that we really begin to understand the heart of God. That's why mercy is one of the rooms we have to pass through on our way to union with Christ.

Even though I have stepped into the room of mercy, it's hard to tell how much progress I've made. Typically, none of us is a very good gauge of our own life, so I'm not sure how far I have come. I do know two things: I'm not where I once was, praise God, but I'm still not where I want to be. Sometimes I feel like I've had to go all the way back to the first door and start over. It seems like I take ten steps forward only to take twelve more backward. There's no need to fear or despair, however. Our Father is gracious. His house has many rooms, and every room leads us closer to Him.

My goal is union with Christ. I've heard it said that walking in the Spirit is walking so close to God as to cast only one shadow—His. That's what I want. When His way and my way are one, the only thing that will be seen is His life. My life will be "hidden with Christ in God."[8]

The Carmelites Are Coming

A few years ago my wife and I led a prayer tour to Israel. One day we found ourselves on the Mount of Olives at the House of Prayer for All Nations, with a dear friend of mine named Tom Hess. Tom lives in Israel and directs this House of Prayer. As we were praying, I felt a bubbling up in my spirit and began to prophesy. I said, "The Carmelites are coming, the Carmelites are coming." At the time I had little idea what it meant. Although I didn't think it was a reference to some kind of candy—"caramel lights" or something—I really had no clue.

A few days later we were on Mount Carmel, where Elijah challenged the 450 priests of Baal in the 18th chapter of First Kings. We were in a prophetic intercessory position, calling for the outpouring of God's Spirit for the next generation of young people in Israel—Jews and Arabs alike—that they may open their eyes and hearts to see Yeshua as their Messiah. While we were praying, a squadron of Israeli fighter jets flew overhead, circling us perhaps seven times, the number of completion.

Several months passed until once again I was with my intercessory friend Tom Hess. He asked me if I remembered my prophecy about the Carmelites. When I told him that I did, he said, "Since you left, a regular prayer gathering has begun on the Mount of Olives that brings together Christian leaders and prayer ministry people from a number of different backgrounds: the Dutch Reformed church, the evangelical church, Charismatics, and Orthodox. There is a group of nuns living near our House of Prayer who are members of an order called the Carmelites. Except for one, they live a cloistered lifestyle, hidden away from others. That one is now praying with us on the Mount of Olives."

Amazed at this confirmation, I exclaimed, "Thank you, God. The Carmelites are coming!"

St. Teresa of Avila—Leader in the
Renewal of Medieval Mysticism

But just who *are* the Carmelites? The Order of Our Lady of Mount Carmel was established in the 12th century. As a mendicant order, the Carmelites combined monastic life with outside religious activity. One tenet of the order was the total renunciation of ownership of either personal or community property.

By the mid-16th century a movement to "bring about personal religious renewal and institutional reform"[9] in the Catholic Church was underway in Europe. This movement, which is known to history as the Catholic Reformation, was parallel to and independent of the more familiar Protestant Reformation.[10] Initially somewhat of a "grass-roots" movement, "these currents of spiritual renewal would not have won the active support of popes and prelates…were it not for the profound shock administered to the church at large by the Protestant Reformation."[11]

> Spain was a major leader in this Catholic renewal, which was characterized by a new flowering of mystical piety… The chief trait of this spirituality was a self-renouncing quietism—a raising of the soul in contemplation and voiceless prayer to God—until a union in divine love, or in ecstasy of inner revelation, was believed to be attained. Prayer is possible only on the basis of self-renunciation, total forgetfulness of self, for God can fill only the soul that has emptied itself of all that is created.[12]

One of the most important and influential figures in this pietistic movement was a Spanish Carmelite nun named Teresa de Cepeda y Ahumada (1515-1582), better known as St. Teresa of Avila. Entering the convent at the age of 20, Teresa battled health problems most of her adult life, particularly during her late twenties. Although she lived a very devout life at the convent, even having several supernatural experiences, in 1555 she underwent what she called a "second conversion" that changed her spiritual life profoundly. Afterwards, her supernatural visions, particularly visions of Christ, occurred more frequently than before.

The Beginning of the Carmelite Houses

Beginning in 1562 and under the guidance of a spiritual counselor, Teresa began establishing new Carmelite houses devoted to the contemplative life. The first of these convents of the Discalced (barefoot) Carmelites was at Avila. "St. Teresa combined intense practicality with the most rarefied spirituality. An excellent and tireless manager, she was endowed with great personal charm, tact, and boundless good nature."[13] She developed quite a following during her lifetime, which was quite unusual for a woman in that day, particularly in the Church. One of her disciples, St. John of the Cross, assisted her in establishing the new Carmelite houses. Today, St. Teresa and St. John of the Cross are regarded as two of the greatest of the Spanish Christian mystics.

Fairly late in her life, and in obedience to instructions from her superiors, Teresa began writing down her mystical and visionary experiences. Although basically uneducated, she proved to have a gift for writing of the spiritual life in simple but eloquent terms. The result is some of the greatest mystical literature ever composed.

Teresa is one of many throughout church history to whom the Lord has given a stewardship of contemplative prayer. She and many others have faithfully kept the watch of quietness before the Lord in waiting upon Him and in sacrificial prayers of fasting, and in quietness before Him have been caught up into the realm of the Spirit to receive those things which only God can give. Teresa of Avila was one of those tender spirits who thought it nothing to waste her life for the Lover of her soul.

The Revelation of the Interior Castle

Teresa's most famous work on prayer is called *The Interior Castle*. Written following an extremely vivid and complex vision, *The Interior Castle* describes the journey of the soul as a progression through a great crystal castle with many rooms, from the outer rooms to the innermost room, where the soul can unite with God completely. The soul makes its way through a series of seven rooms or "mansions," each one bringing it closer and closer to union with God. In colorful and allegorical language, *The Interior Castle* depicts the spiritual journey we all face, with its attendant obstacles and joys. In the words of an editor of Teresa's work, "The figure is used to describe the whole course of the mystical life—the soul's progress from the First Mansions to the Seventh and its transformation from an imperfect and sinful creature into the Bride of the Spiritual Marriage."[14]

When I first discovered *The Interior Castle* a few years ago, I was amazed at the parallels between Teresa's vision of the seven mansions and my own of the seven doorways. I know they are not exactly the same, but the similarities are striking. Teresa saw seven mansions; I saw seven doorways. Teresa saw a progression from room to room in Christian growth from worldliness to holiness and union with Christ; I saw a progression from doorway to doorway of growth in character and grace. In both visions, the progress is toward the ultimate goal of complete union with Christ.

Let's take a closer look at Teresa's vision of *The Interior Castle*.

The First Mansions—the Mansions of Humility

Teresa begins her account by describing the castle and the conditions that exist in the first mansions. The people who enter the first mansions are in the earliest, most basic stages of their Christian walk. They are saved but still retain much of the world's influence.

I began to think of the soul as if it were a castle made of a single diamond or of very clear crystal, in which there were many rooms, just as in Heaven there are many mansions...

Let us now imagine that this castle...contains many mansions, some above, others below, others at each side; and in the center and midst of them all is the chiefest mansion where the most secret things pass between God and the soul...

As far as I can understand, the door of entry into this castle is prayer and meditation: I do not say mental prayer rather than vocal, for, if it is prayer at all, it must be accompanied by meditation...

Let us...think of...souls who do eventually enter the castle. These are very much absorbed in worldly affairs; but their desires are good; sometimes, though infrequently, they commend themselves to Our Lord; and they think about the state of their souls, though not very carefully...Eventually they enter the first rooms on the lowest floor, but so many reptiles [sins and worldly pleasures] get in with them that they are unable to appreciate the beauty of the castle or to find any peace within it.[15]

For Teresa, the key to progress through the first mansions is to learn the lesson of humility. This key to unlock doors is presented over and over again.

In speaking of the soul we must always think of it as spacious, ample, and lofty...for the soul's capacity is much greater than we can realize...It is very important that no soul which practices prayer, whether little or much, should be subjected to undue constraint or limitation. Since God has given it such dignity, it must be allowed to roam through these mansions...It must not be compelled to remain for a long time in one single room—not, at least, unless it is in the room of self-knowledge...Humility must always be doing its work like a bee making its honey in the hive: without humility all will be lost. Still, we should remember that the bee is constantly flying about from flower to flower, and in the same way...the soul must sometimes emerge from self-knowledge and soar aloft in meditation upon the greatness and the majesty of its God...

As I see it, we shall never succeed in knowing ourselves unless we seek to know God: let us think of His greatness and then come back to our own baseness; by looking at His purity we shall see our foulness; by meditating upon His humility, we shall see how far we are from being humble.[16]

The light from the center mansion is dim in the first mansions due both to distance and to the occupants' preoccupation with worldly things. But the farther we proceed with Him, the more light we receive.

The Light **which** comes from the palace occupied by the King hardly reaches these first Mansions at all...not because of anything that is wrong with the room, but rather...because there are so many bad things—snakes and vipers and poisonous creatures—which have come in with the soul that they prevent it from seeing the light.[17]

The Second Mansions—the Mansions of the Practice of Prayer

Those who enter the second mansions have recognized their need to leave the first mansions and, in response to the gentle but persistent call of God, desire to move farther into the castle. They seek out activities and occasions that will advance them in this aim and, because they are beginning to learn how to resist the pull of worldly influences, there is more light and warmth here than in the first mansions.

The souls...that enter the Second Mansions...have already begun to practice prayer and...realize the importance of not remaining in the First Mansions...

These souls, then, can understand the Lord when He calls them; for, as they gradually get nearer to the place where His Majesty dwells, He becomes a very good Neighbor to them. [The] Lord...is so anxious that we should desire Him and strive after His companionship that He calls us ceaselessly, time after time, to approach Him; and this voice of His is so sweet that the poor soul is consumed with grief at being unable to do His bidding immediately...

The will inclines to love One in Whom it has seen so many acts and signs of love, some of which it would like to return.

In particular, the will shows the soul how this true Lover never leaves it, but goes with it everywhere and gives it life and being. Then the understanding comes forward and makes the soul realize that, for however many years it may live, it can never hope to have a better friend.[18]

The Third Mansions—the Mansions of Exemplary Life

The souls who enter the third mansions have grown in spirit to the point where they have developed discipline in their lives and virtue in their behavior. This is a positive step that nevertheless carries the danger of depending on virtuous living rather than on the grace of God. People in the third mansions are governed more by reason and duty than by love. They have not yet made a total surrender in love to God, and therefore experience long periods of dryness in prayer and in other aspects of their Christian lives. (Have you ever visited this room?)

> The souls that have entered the Third Mansions…are most desirous not to offend His Majesty; they avoid committing even venial sins; they love doing penance, they spend hours in recollection; they use their time well; they practice works of charity toward their neighbors; and they are very careful in their speech and dress and in the government of their household if they have one. This is certainly a desirable state and there seems to be no reason why they should be denied entrance to the very last of the Mansions…

> How could anyone ever say that he has no desire for such a wonderful thing…Surely no one could do so. We all say we desire it; but if the Lord is to take complete possession of the soul more than that is necessary. Words are not enough, any more than they were for the young man when the Lord told him what to do if he wished to be perfect. Ever since I began to speak of these Mansions I have had that young man in mind, for we are exactly like him; and this as a rule is the origin of our long periods of aridity in prayer.[19]

The Importance of Humility and Mercy

Again, Teresa stresses the importance of humility, and the recognition that God is sovereign; no matter what we do, God owes us no favors. Anything we receive from Him is purely because of His love, grace, and mercy. Did you catch the word *mercy*? Maybe in my encounter I was seeing more than I had initially perceived.

> It may seem to us that we have done everything...and left all the things of the world and all that we had for His sake...by persevering in this detachment and abandonment of everything, we shall attain our object. But it must be on this condition...**that** we consider ourselves unprofitable servants...and realize that we have in no way obliged our Lord to grant us such favors; but rather that, the more we have received of Him, the more deeply do we remain in His debt...

> What matters is not whether or no we wear a religious habit; it is whether we try to practice the virtues, and make a complete surrender of our wills to God and order our lives as His Majesty ordains: let us desire that not our wills, but His will, be done...

> Those...who, by the goodness of the Lord are in this state...should be studious to render ready obedience.[20]

The Fourth Mansions—the Mansions of the Prayer of Quiet

In the fourth mansions,

> the supernatural element of the mystical life first enters...it is no longer by its own efforts that the soul is acquiring what it gains. Henceforth, the soul's part will become increasing less and God's part increasingly greater. The graces of the fourth mansions, referred to as "spiritual con-solations," are identified with the Prayer of Quiet, or the Second Water, in the Life. The soul is like a fountain built near its source and the water of life flows into it, not through an aqueduct, but directly from the spring.[21]

Teresa gives some sensitive insight into the nature of spiritual love. Now don't give up at this point. Remember, these lovers of God often speak in a romantic hyperbole—poetic nonsense that only the recipient can truly appreciate.

> If you would progress a long way on this road and ascend to the Mansions of your desire, the important thing is not to think much, but to love much; do, then, whatever most arouses you to love...Love consists, not in the extent of our happiness, but in the firmness of our determination to try to

please God in everything, and to endeavor, in all possible ways, not to offend Him...Those are the signs of love; do not imagine that the important thing is never to be thinking of anything else and that if your mind becomes slightly distracted all is lost.[22]

Continuing On to the Prayer of Quiet

One of Teresa's most beautiful images is her description of the consolations of God (also called the Prayer of Quiet) as being like water from a spring. Let this description inspire you to drink from the fountain of God Himself.

Let us suppose that we are looking at two fountains, the basins of which can be filled with water...These two large basins can be filled with water in different ways: the water in the one comes from a long distance, by means of numerous conduits and through human skill; but the other has been constructed at the very source of the water and fills without making any noise. If the flow of water is abundant...a great stream still runs from it after it has been filled; no skill is necessary here, and no conduits have to be made, for the water is flowing all the time. The difference between this and the carrying of the water by means of conduits is, I think, as follows. The latter corresponds to the spiritual sweetness which...is produced by meditation. It reaches us by way of the thoughts...

To the other fountain the water comes direct from its source, which is God, and, when it is His Majesty's will and He is pleased to grant us some supernatural favor, its coming is accompanied by the greatest peace and quietness and sweetness within ourselves—I cannot say where it arises or how. And that content and delight are not felt, as earthly delights are felt, in the heart—I mean not at the outset, for later the basin becomes completely filled, and then this water begins to overflow all the Mansions and faculties, until it reaches the body...

I do not think that this happiness has its source in the heart at all. It arises in a much more interior part, like something of which the springs are very deep; I think this must be the center of the soul...As this heavenly water begins to flow from this source of which I am speaking—that is, from our very depths—it proceeds to spread within us and cause an interior dilation and produce ineffable blessings, so that the soul itself cannot understand all that it receives there.[23]

The Fifth Mansions—the Mansions
of Spiritual Betrothal—the Prayer of Union

The fifth mansions "is the state [of]...Spiritual Betrothal, and the Prayer of Union—that is, incipient Union. It marks a new degree of infused contemplation, and a very high one. By means of the most celebrated of all her metaphors, that of the silkworm, St. Teresa explains how far the soul can prepare itself to receive what is essentially a gift from God."[24] She also describes how the silkworm must die in order to be transformed into a beautiful butterfly. Read slowly and you too will be inspired by this majestic vision.

> The silkworms feed on the mulberry-leaves until they are full-grown, when people put down twigs, upon which, with their tiny mouths, they start spinning silk, making themselves very tight little cocoons, in which they bury themselves. Then, finally, the worm, which was large and ugly, comes right out of the cocoon a beautiful white butterfly...

> The silkworm is like the soul which takes life when, through the heat which comes from the Holy Spirit, it begins to utilize the general help which God gives to us all, and to make use of the remedies which He left in His Church—such as frequent confessions, good books and sermons...The soul begins to live and nourishes itself on this food, and on good meditations, until it is full-grown...When it is full-grown, then...it starts to spin its silk and to build the house in which it is to die. This house may be understood here to mean Christ. I think I read or heard somewhere that our life is hid in Christ, or in God (for that is the same thing), or that our life is Christ...

> May His Majesty Himself be our Mansion as He is in this Prayer of Union...We can neither subtract from, nor add to, God, but we can subtract from, and add to, ourselves, just as these little silkworms do. And, before we have finished doing all that we can in that respect, God will take this tiny achievement of ours, which is nothing at all, unite it with His greatness and give it such worth that its reward will be the Lord Himself...

Let us hasten to perform this task and spin this cocoon. Let us renounce our self-love and self-will, and our attachment to earthly things...Let the silkworm die...Then we shall see God and shall ourselves be as completely hidden in His greatness as is this little worm in its cocoon.[25]

The transformation that occurs after this self-death is truly wondrous.

And now let us see what becomes of this silkworm...When it is in this state of prayer, and quite dead to the world, it comes out a little white butterfly...The soul cannot think how it can have merited such a blessing...It finds itself so anxious to praise the Lord that it would gladly be consumed and die a thousand deaths for His sake. Then it finds itself longing to suffer great trials and unable to do otherwise. It has the most vehement desires for penance, for solitude, and for all to know God. And hence, when it sees God being offended, it becomes greatly distressed...

To see, then, the restlessness of this little butterfly—though it has never been quieter or more at rest in its life! Here is something to praise God for—namely, that it knows not where to settle and make its abode. By comparison with the abode it has had, everything it sees on earth leaves it dissatisfied, especially when God has again and again given it this wine which almost every time has brought it some new blessing. It sets no store by the things it did as a worm— that is, by its gradual weaving of the cocoon. It has wings now: how can it be content to crawl along slowly when it is able to fly?[26]

The Church in Metamorphosis

I too was given a similar, though simpler, vision at one point. In this encounter, the Holy Spirit showed me the work of a caterpillar as it began its process of weaving for itself a cocoon or chrysalis. Soon the caterpillar was no longer in sight, as though hiding. But while it was in this secret place, great change was taking place.

As I continued to watch, I eventually saw something new breaking forth from this clothing of humility. Creating an opening, the new being came forth with feeble wings wet for the wind to dry. Then the butterfly sretched out its wings in full array with irridescent colors brilliantly shimmering.

I asked the Lord, "What is this?" I heard a reply, "This is the Church in metamorphosis." O, may we the Church learn these lessons as taught to St. Teresa and others. May the Bride of Christ—the Church—be adorned with the brilliance of His great presence as we learn once again to abide in the secret place of the Most High.

The Sixth Mansions—the Mansions of Growing Intimacy

The sixth mansions describe the growing intimacy between the soul and God, along with the increasing level of afflictions that attack the soul during this time. As the Lord's favors increase, so do trials and temptations. St. John of the Cross and other mystics referred to this period as "the dark night of the soul." Teresa describes these tribulations as comparable only to those of hell, yet the soul so afflicted desires to escape them only by entering into the final mansions.

> The soul has been wounded with love for the Spouse and seeks more opportunity of being alone, trying, so far as is possible to one in its state, to renounce everything which can disturb it in this its solitude. That sight of Him which it has had is so deeply impressed upon it that its whole desire is to enjoy it once more...

> The soul is now completely determined to take no other spouse; but the Spouse disregards its yearnings for the conclusion of the betrothal, desiring that they should become still deeper and that this greatest of all blessings should be won by the soul at some cost to itself...Oh, my God, how great are these trials, which the soul will suffer, both within and without, before it enters the Seventh Mansion!...

> For often when a person is quite unprepared for such a thing, and is not even thinking of God, he is awakened by His Majesty, as though by a rushing comet or a thunderclap. Although no sound is heard, the soul is very well aware that it has been called by God...It is conscious of having been most delectably wounded, but cannot say how or by whom; but it is certain that this is a precious experience and it would be glad if it were never to be healed of that wound. It complains to its Spouse with words of love, and even cries aloud, being unable to help itself, for it realizes that He is present but will not manifest Himself in such a way as to allow it to enjoy Him...For the Spouse, Who is in

the Seventh Mansion, seems to be calling the soul in a way which involves no clear utterance of speech.[27]

The Favors Granted

During the Sixth Mansions, Teresa describes many kinds of "favors" that the Spouse bestows on His Beloved, such as raptures, flights of the soul, transports of the mind into states of ecstasy, etc. These only make the pain of separation more exquisite for the soul, and increases its desire for oneness with the Spouse. Sounds inviting to me!

> Have all these favors which the Spouse has granted the soul been sufficient to satisfy this little…butterfly…and to make her settle down in the place where she is to die? Certainly not; she is in a much worse state than before; for, although she may have been receiving these favors for many years, she is still sighing and weeping, and each of them cause her fresh pain. The reason for this is that, the more she learns about the greatness of her God, while finding herself so far from Him and unable to enjoy Him, the more her desire increases. For the more is revealed to her of how much this great God and Lord deserves to be loved, the more does her love for Him grow. And gradually, during these years, her desire increases, so that she comes to experience great distress.[28]

The Seventh Mansions—the Mansions of Spiritual Marriage

Finally, at long last and after many trials, the soul enters the seventh mansions, the dwelling place of the King. Here, there is "complete transformation, ineffable and perfect peace; no higher state is conceivable, save that of the Beatific Vision in the life to come."[29]

> When Our Lord is pleased to have pity upon this soul, which suffers and has suffered so much out of desire for Him, and which He has now taken spiritually to be His bride, He brings her into this Mansion of His, which is the seventh, before consummating the Spiritual Marriage. For He must needs have an abiding-place in the soul, just as He has one in Heaven, where His Majesty alone dwells…this secret union takes place in the deepest center of the soul, which must be where God Himself dwells…The Lord appears in the center of the soul…just as He appeared to the Apostles, without entering through the door…This instantaneous

communication of God to the soul is so great a secret and so sublime a favor, and such delight is felt by the soul, that I do not know with what to compare it, beyond saying that the Lord is pleased to manifest to the soul at that moment the glory that is in Heaven...

We might say that union is as if the ends of two wax candles were joined so that the light they give is one...it is like rain falling from the heavens into a river or spring; there is nothing but water there and it is impossible to divide or separate the water belonging to the river from that which fell from the heavens. Or it is as if a tiny streamlet enters the sea, from which it will find no way of separating itself, or as if in a room there were two large windows through which the light streamed in: it enters in different places but it all becomes one.[30]

A Love Beyond Words

Many Christians today would find Teresa's mystical imagery difficult to understand because the intensity of her experiential focus is so foreign to them. They would also feel distinctly uncomfortable with the intimate "bedroom" language she uses to describe her experience. What other kind of words can you use to try and articulate the most intimate love relationship you have ever known?

So now we come to the end of our first section of *Wasted on Jesus*—"The Inward Journey: Proceeding Into His Presence"—only to find that it is just a beginning. We have ventured deep into the center of our Father's house and seen for ourselves that indeed it has "many rooms."

I want to say to you that there is a room tailor-made for each of us, and the Lord bids us to sit and rest and wait—as Mary of Bethany did at the feet of Jesus; as John laid his head on His breast; as Lydia opened her heart—and learn from Him. No words are necessary. It is a quiet place, far from the madding crowd, where we can satisfy our hunger with the bread of Heaven and slake our thirst at the wellsprings of the water of Life. As we rest and wait, He leads us into the quietness of the soul. This restful place of waiting on Him is another means of expressing our extravagant love being wasted only on Him.

Reflection Questions

1. Describe what is meant by the Scripture, "you are a temple of God."

2. Are there any rooms in your house that need to be cleaned out? If so, which ones?

3. Which rooms do you like staying in for awhile—the rooms in your house that you and God are most comfortable with?

Recommended Reading

The Interior Castle by St. Teresa of Avila (Image/Doubleday, 1989)

Devotional Classics by Richard Foster and James Bryant Smith (Harper Collins, 1993)

Radiant Glory: The Life of Martha Wing Robinson (Bread of Life, 1962)

Endnotes

1. Col. 1:27b.
2. 1 Cor. 3:17b.
3. 1 Cor. 6:19.
4. 2 Cor. 6:16b.
5. 1 Pet. 2:4-5.
6. Jn. 14:1-3.
7. Mt. 5:3.
8. Col. 3:3b.
9. Williston Walker, Richard A. Norris, David W. Lotz, and Richard T. Handy, *A History of the Christian Church*, 4th ed., New York, NY: Scribner, a trademark of Simon and Shuster, 1985, p. 502.
10. *Ibid.*
11. *Ibid.*
12. *Ibid.*, p. 513.
13. Tommy Tenney, *God's Favorite House Journal*, Shippensburg, PA: Fresh Bread, an Imprint of Destiny Image Publishers, Inc., 2000, p. 65.
14. P. Silverio de Stanta Teresa, from the introduction to *The Interior Castle* by St. Teresa of Avila, <http://www. ccel.org/t/teresa/castle/castle.html> 28 Sept. 2000.
15. Teresa of Avila, *The Interior Castle*, <http://www.ccel.org/t/teresa/castle/castle.html> 28 Sept. 2000
16. *Ibid.*
17. *Ibid.*
18. *Ibid.*
19. *Ibid.*
20. *Ibid.*
21. P. Silverio, introduction to *The Interior Castle*.
22. Teresa of Avila, *The Interior Castle*.
23. *Ibid.*
24. P. Silverio, introduction to *The Interior Castle*.
25. Teresa of Avila, *The Interior Castle*.
26. *Ibid.*
27. *Ibid.*
28. *Ibid.*
29. P. Silverio, introduction to *The Interior Castle*.
30. Teresa of Avila, *The Interior Castle*.

Part Two

The Quietness of the Soul: Waiting on Him

Chapter Five

By the Quiet Stream

There's a lot of talk these days about the "river"—those external swells of God's presence that just keep coming and coming, breaking over His people in engulfing billows of divine love and refreshing. I love being in the "river" as much as anyone. It feels great to drink of the running water of the Lord and to be refreshed and filled to overflowing in the Spirit. However, there is another source of spiritual water that I love just as much as the external "river" of God.

I grew up in a tiny town in Missouri with a population of less than 300. I was actually even born at home, my birth attended by the local doctor and neighbor midwife down the street. During my early childhood years, we had no indoor plumbing in our house. Instead, we drew all of our water from an outside well that was capped with a manual pump. No matter how hot a day it might be, that well water drawn from deep within the earth was always cool and refreshing. I have vivid memories of cranking that pump handle and watching the life-giving water splash into the bucket.

As Christians we are like wells in many ways. Deep inside each of us is a "room"—a "springhouse" if you will—that contains a never-ending supply of "living water." Its source is God Himself. This is the kind of water Jesus was talking about when He said to the Samaritan woman at Jacob's well, "whoever drinks of the water that I will give him shall never thirst; but the water that I will give him will become in him a well of water springing up to eternal life."[1] When we draw that water up from the depths of our soul—when we "fill our bucket"—it renews, refreshes, and revitalizes not only us, but also everyone with whom we share it.

The Lord tells us in Isaiah that we "will joyously draw water from the springs of salvation."[2] A spring is an opening in the earth where subterranean water bubbles up spontaneously and flows onto the ground. In John 7:38, Jesus prophesied that "rivers of living water" would flow from the hearts of those who believe in Him. He was referring to the wellspring of the Holy Spirit, who would later be given to His disciples. Even the greatest rivers begin as small, seemingly insignificant springs.

We Must Go *Inward* in Order to Go *Outward*

For me, the well is a picture of what contemplative prayer is like. As I quiet my soul being before God, I lower my "bucket" into the depths of my inner being, where He fills it with His living water. Then I raise my bucket so His water can nourish my spirit and overflow to others as well. I have to go *inward* in order to go *outward*. I believe experientially that this is part of what it means to have "Christ in you, the hope of glory."[3]

Once we learn to tap into this inner spiritual well of quietness and contemplation in the very presence of our Beloved, we will discover a source of peace, strength, and stability that the world knows nothing about. We find this theme over and over in Isaiah.

- *You will keep him in perfect peace, whose mind is stayed on You, because he trusts in You.*[4]

- *In repentance and rest you will be saved, in quietness and trust is your strength.*[5]

- *Do you not know? Have you not heard? The Everlasting God, the Lord, the Creator of the ends of the earth does not become weary or tired. His understanding is inscrutable. He gives strength to the weary, and to him who lacks might He increases power. Though youths grow weary and tired, and vigorous young men stumble badly, yet those who wait for the Lord will gain new strength; they will mount up with wings like eagles, they will run and not get tired, they will walk and not become weary.*[6]

The way we tap into this source of inner life, peace, strength, and confidence is by learning to quiet ourselves and wait on the Lord. To put it another way, we need to learn *how to practice the presence of God* in our daily lives. One of my favorite prayer postures is sitting with a blanket over my head as a tool of helping me remove as many external distractions as possible, quiet my spirit, and commune silently with the God who lives within me. There is a time and place for aggressive postures in intercession and spiritual warfare, but I have discovered that my effectiveness in going *outward* is directly proportional to how deeply I am maintaining my *inward* devotional Mary position.

Jesus told His disciples, "In that day you will know that I am in My Father, and you in Me, and I in you."[7] Even though Jesus is seated at the right hand of the Father, He has also taken up His abode, through the Holy Spirit, in the heart of every born-again believer. The Lord of glory has chosen to dwell in these "clay pots" of ours so that out of them can shine the glorious light of His manifested presence. As we go inward in growing communion with Him, we learn how to call forth the living water within us and release it in an outward flood that transforms lives and nations.

Going Inward Helps Us Learn to Stay Our Minds on Jesus

Martha Wing Robinson was a pioneer in the Pentecostal movement who was personally well acquainted with this inward journey. The founder of the Zion Faith Home in Zion, Illinois, she was known as a woman through whom the presence of God shown radiantly. Here are her thoughts on "inwardness."

> When Jesus first sets vessels to love Him, He wants them to see Him all the time, every moment, and if they are very much in earnest, to live that way—moment by moment.

> In the beginning of such experience, most of the time they pray, praise, wait on God, commune, and often, if at work, see Jesus in the soul.

> If they grow in this experience and become vessels of God for His use, they begin to seek more for Him, and He comes more to them, for He does to all who seek Him from the heart.

> Also, He begins to draw their thoughts all the time—every moment—to Himself, causing them to find Him within. This is the beginning of the inward or deeper life.

> As soon as this change takes place, He then teaches, if He can make them to get it, either by teachers or by their light, how to "practice the presence of God"—that is, to keep the mind *stayed* on Jesus—each wandering thought, act, word,

or feeling being recalled, (i.e. called back) by the will of the vessel in the love of God.

However, this takes care. Often the mind lingers over a subject not of God. Turn the mind back to God. Words come not appointed by Him. Check such words at once, as soon as remembered. Look within and tell Jesus He rules, you will act, think and speak as He would, and He will look after you to help you to be like that.

Also, you need to watch and to pray to be in God, wait in God, etc. To so live for a time makes the inward change to abide in anyone who will go down to thus live; but if you keep to this lowliness, rest, and faith to be all the time in God so, then the voluntary act of dwelling in God, seeing God, thinking of God, and keeping in is done altogether by the Holy Ghost, which is the true inwardness called for in every Christian.[8]

David, the Shepherd-King of Israel, Knew the Presence of God

Practicing the presence of God, dwelling in God, seeing God, thinking of God—all of these are descriptions of contemplative prayer and waiting in quietness before the Lord. David, the Shepherd-King of Israel, knew this way intimately; his psalms clearly attest to that fact. I am constantly inspired and encouraged by the life and example of David. If someone as thoroughly human and flawed as he could enjoy intimate fellowship with God, then I know there is hope for all of us! David made many mistakes—he was an adulterer, a murderer, and a less than effective father—yet in spite of these failings, he was a man of great faith who loved the Lord with all his heart.

God had chosen David to replace the disobedient Saul as king of Israel. When Samuel confronted Saul about his disobedience, he told the king, "But now your kingdom shall not endure. The Lord has sought out for Himself a man after His own heart, and the Lord has appointed him as ruler over His people, because you have not kept what the Lord commanded you."[9] That man was David. The phrase "after His own heart" is a beautiful description of a person who enjoys an intimate relationship with God, and it fit David perfectly.

From what we can tell of his life from the Scriptures and of his heart as revealed in his psalms, David apparently enjoyed a personal relationship with God that was leagues ahead of others of his day in intimacy and spiritual understanding. Just a sampling from the Psalms reveals the power and quality of this relationship from David's perspective.

In the morning, O Lord, You will hear my voice; in the morning I will order my prayer to You and eagerly watch.[10]

Make me know Your ways, O Lord; teach me Your paths. Lead me in Your truth and teach me, for You are the God of my salvation; for You I wait all the day.[11]

One thing I have asked from the Lord, that I shall seek: that I may dwell in the house of the Lord all the days of my life, to behold the beauty of the Lord and to meditate in His temple.[12]

I will bless the Lord at all times; His praise shall continually be in my mouth. My soul will make its boast in the Lord; the humble will hear it and rejoice. O magnify the Lord with me, and let us exalt His name together...O taste and see that the Lord is good; how blessed is the man who takes refuge in Him![13]

Behold, God is my helper; the Lord is the sustainer of my soul.[14]

For You have been a refuge for me, a tower of strength against the enemy. Let me dwell in Your tent forever; let me take refuge in the shelter of Your wings.[15]

My soul waits in silence for God only; from Him is my salvation.[16]

God, You are my God; I shall seek You earnestly; my soul thirsts for You, my flesh yearns for You, in a dry and weary land where there is no water...Because Your lovingkindness is better than life, my lips will praise You...When I remember You on my bed, I meditate on You in the night watches.[17]

Teach me Your way, O Lord; I will walk in Your truth; unite my heart to fear Your name.[18]

Lord, You have searched me and known me. You know when I sit down and when I rise up; You understand my thought from afar. You scrutinize my path and my lying down, and are intimately acquainted with all my ways...How precious also are Your thoughts to me, O God! How vast is the sum of them!...Search me, O God, and know my heart; try me and know my anxious thoughts; and see if there be any hurtful way in me, and lead me in the everlasting way.[19]

I remember the days of old; I meditate on all Your doings; I muse on the work of Your hands. I stretch out my hands to You; my soul longs for You, as a parched land.[20]

On the glorious splendor of Your majesty and on Your wonderful works, I will meditate.[21]

David Knew the Joy of Intimate Love With His Shepherd

Without a doubt, Psalm 23 is the masterpiece of all the word-pictures that hang in the gallery of David's portraits of his relationship with God. For nearly three thousand years this psalm has encouraged the living, strengthened the dying, and comforted the grieving. While it is certainly appropriate for all of these, I believe that it is even more appropriate to view this psalm as a picture of our life with God in the here-and-now. David lived in an intimate love relationship with God. That relationship grew out of a lifelong practice of worship, prayer, and quiet contemplation, which David first learned during long nights in the fields near Bethlehem keeping his father's sheep. The bond between the Shepherd and His sheep that David depicts in the 23rd Psalm is a beautiful picture of the love and trust that exist between the Lord and those whom He draws to Himself. For David, it was a description of his life eagerly "wasted" on adoration and devotion for the Lover and Satisfier of his soul.

"The Lord is my shepherd, I shall not want." At the outset, David states the nature of the relationship clearly and plainly. The Lord *is* his shepherd; there is no doubt or uncertainty here. He who had been a shepherd himself now wrote from the perspective of a sheep. In the natural, sheep are totally dependent on their shepherd for food, water, shelter, safety—even life itself. Basically, they are helpless, needy creatures. In the spiritual, we humans are just as helpless and dependent on God as sheep are on their shepherd. In many ways, we are also just as needy, because so many of us so often fail to recognize or acknowledge how dependent we are on the Lord for everything.

This is also a statement of ownership. If the Lord is our shepherd, that means He *owns* us. He has bought us with a price. The tenth chapter of John depicts Jesus as the "good shepherd" who gives His life for His sheep.[22] He bought us with His own blood; we now belong to Him. This fact of divine ownership was a source of great joy and confidence for David, just as it should be for us. The great British preacher Charles Spurgeon explained it this way:

David...compares himself to a creature weak, defenseless, and foolish, and he takes God to be his Provider, Preserver, Director, and, indeed, his everything. No man has a right to consider himself the Lord's sheep unless his nature has been renewed, for the scriptural description of unconverted men does not picture them as sheep, but as wolves or goats. A sheep is an object of property, not a wild animal; its owner sets great store by it, and frequently it is bought with a great price. It is well to know, as certainly as David did, that we belong to the Lord. There is a noble tone of confidence about this sentence. There is no "if" nor "but," nor even "I hope so," but he says, "The Lord *is* my shepherd."[23]

Phillip Keller, in his devotional classic *A Shepherd Looks at Psalm 23*, writes, "David...spoke with a strong sense of pride and devotion and admiration. It was as though he literally boasted aloud, 'Look at who my shepherd is—my owner—my manager!' The Lord is!"[24] It is when we are in that quiet place of fellowship with God and commune with Him spirit to Spirit that "The Spirit Himself testifies with our spirit that we are children of God."[25]

David knew that with the Lord as his shepherd, his every need would be provided, so he could proclaim with confidence, "I shall not want." Whether temporal or spiritual, every need we have will be supplied by our Shepherd, the great Lover of our soul, if we trust Him. Phillip Keller says that the word *want* here has a broader meaning than simply not lacking anything. It also carries the idea of "being utterly contented in the Good Shepherd's care and consequently not craving or desiring anything more."[26] Our Shepherd supplies more than just our daily needs; He supplies us with *Himself*. When the Lord is our shepherd, He fills us with His presence and satisfies our deepest longings and greatest yearnings, so that we no longer need or want anything or anyone but Him. He satisfies us because, as someone said years ago, He fills the "God-shaped void" in each of us that only He can fill.

As we sit and wait on the Lord in the quietness of our soul, one of the things He teaches us is that when we have Him, we have *everything*—period. There is nothing more we need. No one else can satisfy us completely, body, soul, and spirit, the way He can. Something I learned long ago from some of the veterans of the walk with the Lord is that the farther we go in Christ, the simpler we become, and the clearer our focus that Jesus is all. The deepest yet simplest truth in all of Scripture is Jesus Christ, crucified and risen. That says it all. He is it. Jesus is our everything. In Him we are complete. It is hard for us to understand that—or truly believe it—until we have learned to separate ourselves mentally and emotionally from the attractions and distractions of the world. When the Lord calls us away to that quiet place where we can hear His "still, small voice," it is then that we know, beyond doubt, that He is all we need. It is in that place that you become "wasted by Him" and then in turn want to "waste a life on Jesus!"

David Knew the Peace of Green Pastures and Quiet Waters

He makes me lie down in green pastures; He leads me beside quiet waters. As a shepherd, David knew the importance of providing abundant forage and fresh, clean water for his flocks. Sheep thrive best in dry, semi-arid climates, but sufficient supplies of "green pastures" and "quiet waters" can be difficult to find under those conditions. It is the shepherd's responsibility to know where these places are and to lead his flocks safely to them. As a sheep of the Good Shepherd, David expressed complete confidence and contentment in his Shepherd's provision and care. This is a trust born of intimate friendship.

More lies behind David's words than meets the eye. Leading the flocks to green pastures and quiet waters requires patient, constant attention by the shepherd. Phillip Keller provides some interesting insights on the peculiar needs of sheep.

> The strange thing about sheep is that because of their very make-up it is almost impossible for them to be made to lie down unless four requirements are met.
>
> Owing to their timidity they refuse to lie down unless they are free of all fear.
>
> Because of the social behavior within a flock sheep will not lie down unless they are free from friction with others of their kind.
>
> If tormented by flies or parasites, sheep will not lie down. Only when free of these pests can they relax.
>
> Lastly, sheep will not lie down as long as they feel in need of finding food. They must be free from hunger.
>
> It is significant that to be at rest there must be a definite sense of freedom from fear, tension, aggravations and hunger. The unique aspect of the picture is that it is only the

sheepman himself who can provide release from these anxieties. It all depends upon the diligence of the owner whether or not his flock is free of disturbing influences.[27]

The Benefits

The "disturbing influences" of "fear, tension, aggravations and hunger" fade into the background when, waiting in the quietness of our spirit, we contemplate the face and character of our Shepherd, the Lover of our soul. He leads us to the nourishing green pastures of His Word and the quiet waters of His Spirit where we find rest for our souls. In that place He strengthens us and restores us, and bathes us in His love, not just for our own sake, but for His, that we might be renewed and equipped to bring other sheep into His fold.

Charles Spurgeon, who certainly was well acquainted with the ways of his Shepherd, wrote:

> The Christian life has two elements in it, the contemplative and the active, and both of these are richly provided for. First, the contemplative, "*He maketh me to lie down in green pastures.*" What are these "*green pastures*" but the Scriptures of truth—always fresh, always rich, and never exhausted?...Sweet and full are the doctrines of the gospel; fit food for souls, as tender grass is natural nutriment for sheep. When by faith we are enabled to find rest in the promises, we are like the sheep that lie down in the midst of the pasture...

> The second part of a vigorous Christian's life consists in gracious activity. We not only think, but we act. We are not always lying down to feed, but are journeying onward toward perfection; hence we read, "*he leadeth me beside the still waters.*" What are these "*still waters*" but the influences and graces of his blessed Spirit? His Spirit attends us in various operations, like waters—in the plural to cleanse, to refresh, to fertilize, to cherish. They are "*still* waters," for the Holy Ghost loves peace, and sounds no trumpet of ostentation in his operations...

> "In sacred silence of the mind

> My heaven, and there my God I find"...

> Still waters run deep...That silence is golden indeed in which the Holy Spirit meets with the souls of his saints. Not

to raging waves of strife, but to peaceful streams of holy love does the Spirit of God conduct the chosen sheep...Our Lord leads us beside these *"still waters"*; we could not go there of ourselves, we need his guidance, therefore is it said, *"he leadeth me."*[28]

Just as Martha's busy serving and Mary's quiet sitting were both acceptable to the Lord,[29] so contemplation and action are two sides of the same coin. A healthy Christian life needs both. Nathanael Hardy, a biblical scholar of an earlier generation, wrote: "Sitting Mary and stirring Martha are emblems of contemplation and action, and as they dwell in one house, so must these in one heart."[30] Contemplation is *inward*, action is *outward*. Inward contemplation that does not issue forth in outward action will become stagnant and lifeless, like the water in the Dead Sea, because it has no outlet. On the other hand, outward action that is not preceded by inward contemplation will be devoid of revelation.

Quietness is the incubator for the Spirit of revelation. Do you want to hear God better? Do you want to commune with Him more? Then trust the Good Shepherd and lie down in His green pastures and rest by His quiet waters.

We Will Never Rest Until We Find Our Rest in God

Sitting by the quiet stream is one of the best medicines for our fast-paced, helter-skelter, microwave society. Simplicity and solitude are lost arts in our culture, even among Christians, which is one reason why so many believers complain that God seems so distant and unreal to them. We need a renewed emphasis on this facet of our spiritual lives. It's time to rediscover the power of contemplation, return to the quiet stream, and let the Good Shepherd restore our souls.

Have you gone on a walk and then sat down on a creek bed or the side of a crystal clear stream? The next thing you do is to take your shoes off and dip your feet into the flowing cool waters. At first, it might seem too extreme of a difference in temperature to your feet. But after awhile, not only do you get used to it, the soles of your feet are being soothed by the quiet babbling stream. It's more than a "Kodak moment"; it can be a real life experience.

Yes, He leads us besides the quiet stream. It is there that He restores our soul. Need cooled off? Just push that pause button again for a moment and dip your soul into the ocean of His great love and rest for a bit. Then you will be renewed to get back up and begin another leg of your journey.

Rest—the Passageway to Intimacy

David's life was full of ups and downs, mountains and valleys. He sinned great sins, but found greater forgiveness. For the most part he ruled wisely and well, but at times displayed shocking foolishness. He suffered family dysfunction, division, intrigue, rebellion, and tragedy, yet was succeeded on the throne by a beloved son who became the wisest man who ever lived. Through it all, David's heart remained steadfastly fixed on his Shepherd, the Lover of his soul, who had called him out of his father's fields to "shepherd" the nation of Israel. As a result, David enjoyed an intimacy and communion with God unlike that experienced by any others of his day.

What did all of this mean to David? How did he feel about his relationship with God? I think one of his most beautiful descriptions is found in the 16th Psalm:

> *The Lord is the portion of my inheritance and my cup; You support my lot. The lines have fallen to me in pleasant places; indeed, my heritage is beautiful to me. I will bless the Lord who has counseled me; indeed my mind instructs me in the night. I have set the Lord continually before me; because He is at my right hand, I will not be shaken. Therefore my heart is glad and my glory rejoices; my flesh also will dwell securely. For You will not abandon my soul to Sheol; nor will You allow Your Holy One to undergo decay. You will make known to me the path of life; in Your presence is fullness of joy; in Your right hand there are pleasures forever.*[31]

I once asked my good friend Mahesh Chavda, "Mahesh, I know you hear the voice of the Spirit of God. How does it come to you; what is it like?"

He chuckled and said, "Jim, the closer I get to Him, the gentler His voice becomes."

That is so true. The closer we get to the Lord, the gentler His voice becomes. The more we learn how to listen, the easier it becomes to hear Him speak. It is always a faith walk. Sometimes we may feel like nothing is happening, but the reality is that we are soaking up His presence. Then, when we least expect it, at God's appointed time He "opens the valve," and floods of blessing and glory come gushing out of us that we had no idea had even been deposited there.

I think David summed it up well when he wrote, "Rest in the Lord; wait patiently for him to act...Don't fret and worry—it only leads to harm...But all who humble themselves before the Lord shall be given every blessing and shall have wonderful peace."[32]

God created us for intimate relationship with Him, and we will never be satisfied with anything less. David knew this; that's why he loved and pursued God with all his heart. The Lord has called us to do the same. That is our purpose and our destiny. Perhaps no one stated this better than St. Augustine:

O God! Thou hast made us for Thyself and our souls are restless, searching, 'til they find their rest in Thee.[33]

Jesus said it this way, "The foxes have holes and the birds of the air have nests, but the Son of Man has nowhere to lay His head" (Mt. 8:20). It is true, we will never truly rest till we find our rest in God. But there is another truth also. We are to be His resting place.

Come join me by the quiet stream and let's give Him a place where He can rest His head—even on His beloved!

Reflection Questions

1. Did you ever put your feet in a cool stream or body of water? What did it do for you?
2. When you go to pray, how do you handle distractions?
3. What did Jesus mean by His statement, "From [your] innermost being will flow rivers of living water"?

Recommended Reading

A Shepherd Looks at the Twenty-third Psalm by Phillip Keller (Zondervan Publishing House, 1970)
Consecrated Contemplative Prayer by Jim W. Goll (Ministry to the Nations, 2000)
Enjoying the Presence of God by Martyn Lloyd-Jones (Servant, 1991)

Endnotes

1. Jn. 4:14.
2. Is. 12:3.
3. Col. 1:27b.
4. Is. 26:3 NKJ.
5. Is. 30:15.
6. Is. 40:28-31.
7. Jn. 14:20.
8. From a teaching of the Zion Faith Home, Zion, Illinois.
9. 1 Sam. 13:14.
10. Ps. 5:3.
11. Ps. 25:4-5.
12. Ps. 27:4.
13. Ps. 34:1-3, 8.
14. Ps. 54:4.

15. Ps. 61:3-4.
16. Ps. 62:1.
17. Ps. 63:1, 3, 6.
18. Ps. 86:11.
19. Ps. 139:1-3, 17, 23-24.
20. Ps. 143:5-6.
21. Ps. 145:5.
22. Jn. 10:11.
23. Charles H. Spurgeon, *The Treasury of David*, Psalms 1-57, Electronic Edition STEP Files, Hiawatha, IA: Parsons Technology, Inc., 1997.
24. Phillip Keller, *A Shepherd Looks at Psalm 23*, Grand Rapids, MI: Zondervan Publishing House, 1970, p. 17.
25. Rom. 8:16.
26. Keller, *A Shepherd Looks at Psalm 23*, p. 26.
27. *Ibid.*, pp. 35-36.
28. Spurgeon, *The Treasury of David*, Psalms 1-57.
29. Lk. 10:38-42.
30. Nathanael Hardy, quoted in Spurgeon, *The Treasury of David*, Psalms 1-57.
31. Ps. 16:5-11.
32. Ps. 37:7a, 8b, 11 LB.
33. St. Augustine, quoted in Keller, *A Shepherd Looks at Psalm 23*, p. 51.

Chapter Six

The Center of Quiet

A hurricane is one of the most dangerous and destructive forces of nature on earth. Torrential rains coupled with winds that often exceed two hundred miles an hour can completely devastate islands or coastal regions over which they pass. The loss of human life can be horrific. In 1900 a hurricane slammed into the island community of Galveston, Texas, laying waste to most of the island. Caught unprepared, as many as ten thousand or more of the residents of Galveston were swept away by the storm.

One of the peculiar features of a hurricane is the eye, a hub of calm around which the swirling winds and driving rains rotate. Many people who have gone through a hurricane have described the eye as a period of eerie, almost unearthly calm. The winds suddenly die down, the rain stops, the sky clears, and there is a period of stillness for several hours until the back side of the storm passes over, kicking the wind and rain up again in the opposite direction as before.

Just as in the natural there is an eye, or center, of quiet in the midst of every hurricane, so it is in the realm of the Spirit. There is a refuge to which we can turn from the storms and pressures of life. Just as there was a progression in Moses' tabernacle from the outer court to the Most Holy Place, so there is within every believer a progression through the tempests of life into a place of quiet communion in the Spirit. That is the place where God dwells, and in Him there is perfect peace.

But how do we get there? How do we pass through the turmoil of our minds and the busyness of our lives to enter the center of quiet? I have already dealt with this to some degree in earlier chapters, but here I want to talk about some more practical aspects of the process. Although ultimately it is the Lord Himself who through His Spirit draws us into the center of quiet with Him, there are specific things we can do to help prepare ourselves physically and mentally to enter into the contemplative state.

There Are Five Essential Ingredients of the Contemplative-Meditative State

In their wonderful book *Communion with God*, Mark and Patti Virkler give some very practical guidelines for learning how to enter the meditative state. These guidelines address the physical, mental, and spiritual aspects of preparation.

> The five key ingredients of the contemplative or meditative state are physical calm, focused attention, letting be, receptivity and spontaneous flow. The opposites of these characteristics are physical tension, distraction, over-control, activity, and analytical thought…
>
> Meditation is commanded throughout the Scriptures, and so are each of these elements that make up the meditative pose.[1]

The first ingredient is *physical calm*.[2] "There remains a Sabbath rest for the people of God. For the one who has entered His rest has himself also rested from his works, as God did from His. Therefore let us be diligent to enter that rest, so that no one will fall, through following the same example of disobedience."[3] "And to whom did He swear that they would not enter His rest, but to those who were disobedient? So we see that they were not able to enter because of unbelief."[4] Entering into God's rest requires both faith and obedience. Physical calm is an important place to start. It won't happen by itself; we must be deliberate about it. Some characteristics of being physically calm are a steady, even heartbeat; calm, easy breathing; relaxed muscles; and lack of tension.

Focused attention is the next element of the contemplative state. "Let us…lay aside every encumbrance and…sin which so easily entangles us, and let us run…fixing our eyes on Jesus, the author and perfecter of faith…"[5] "Truly, truly I say to you, the Son can do nothing of Himself, unless it is something He sees the Father doing; for whatever the Father does, these things the Son also does in like manner."[6] We are to fix the eyes of our heart firmly upon Jesus Christ, the Lover of our soul. Features of focused attention include ordered thoughts; a clear, steady and focused mind that is not easily distracted; and clear priorities and goals.

The third component of the meditative state is *letting be*. "Cease striving and know that I am God."[7] "Be anxious for nothing, but in everything by prayer and supplication with thanksgiving let your requests be made known to God. And the peace of God, which surpasses all comprehension, will guard your hearts and your minds in Christ Jesus."[8] Characteristics of letting be include not being driven by our desires, being able to let go mentally of problems or situations that we have no direct or immediate control over, and being patient.

Receptivity is the fourth element of the contemplative posture. "Abide in Me, and I in you. As the branch cannot bear fruit of itself unless it abides in the vine, so neither can you unless you abide in Me. I am the vine, you are the branches; he who abides in Me and I in him, he bears much fruit, for apart from Me you can do nothing."[9] The only way we can be and remain receptive to the Lord is to stay "stuck" to Him. Qualities of receptiveness include an awareness of God flowing through us; recognition that all our ability, strength, wisdom, and understanding come from God; and a sense of complete dependence upon the Holy Spirit in day to day living.

The final ingredient of the meditative state is *spontaneous flow*. " 'He who believes in Me, as the Scripture said, "From his innermost being will flow rivers of living water."' But this He spoke of the Spirit, whom those who believed in Him who were to receive..."[10] This river of living water has its source in God Himself, but it will flow spontaneously from within us just as a natural river flows spontaneously from a spring. Characteristics of spontaneous flow include a sensitivity to and willingness to follow inner promptings, awareness of creative expression flowing within, and being uncomfortable living in "boxes."

God has placed a river of living water—His Spirit—inside each of us. He wants that river to pour forth from us even more than we want it to. The way we tap into that river is by entering the center of quiet. There we can pray that not a trickle but a gusher of living water will pour out, that we might be a well-watered garden, and a pool of refreshing where others can come and renew themselves in the life-giving flow of the Lord.

Prayer Is Becoming Friends With God

Any friendship goes through different stages in its development. The same is true with our friendship with God; we move to progressively higher and deeper levels toward the goal of perfect union with Christ. This was the whole theme of St. Teresa of Avila's *The Interior Castle.*

Perhaps we could define prayer as "two lovers sharing love together."[11] If that sounds shockingly intimate, it may be because we still have trouble thinking of God in such a personal way or regarding our relationship with Him as a love relationship. Many Christians don't feel like God *really* loves them. If you are one of them, let me assure you that the opposite is true. God loves you much more than you can possibly comprehend. His love for all of us is boundless. One of the glories of Heaven will be the opportunity to spend an eternity getting to know the eternal love of our eternal God!

In the meantime, we have the chance while on earth to become *friends* with God. Some have identified five stages of friendship[12] which are true whether we are talking about human relationships or our friendship with God. Stage one is the *casual* stage, where we speak about general things: sports, the weather, hobbies, politics, etc. It's basically superficial talk, but laying the foundation for a deeper relationship. The second stage is the stage of *beginning trust*, where we first begin to share some of our personal thoughts and feelings. As the friendship continues to develop, we progress to stage three, *deep trust*. This is the level where we share our dreams, our mistakes, and our frustrations. The friendship is deep enough that we can trust our friend with our vulnerabilities. At stage four we enter true *intimacy* for the first time, sitting quietly with our Friend and experiencing a Presence that is beyond words. The final stage is *union*, where we become one with our Friend, feeling as He feels and acting as He acts.

Jesus said, "No longer do I call you slaves, for the slave does not know what his master is doing; but I have called you friends, for all things that I have heard from My Father I have made known to you."[13] What an awesome blessing and privilege it is to be called the Lord's *friends*! We come to know our greatest Friend through prayer. As Mark and Patti Virkler say, "Prayer is not doing something, but being with Someone until I become one with Him, until I become the expression of Jesus."[14]

Another way to describe prayer is that it is desire expressed. In every petition, in every intercession, in all our pleading and reminding God of His Word, let us be sure to "let [our] requests be made known to God," expressing our desire for greater friendship with Him.

At all times we should continue to hold onto His hand upward as we reach out in faith outward. What this means is that as we hold on to the upward hand of God in friendship, we have safety, security, power and confidence to go forth in the outward expressions of ministry.

Jesus Knew the Value of Solitude

Another way to refer to the "center of quiet" is to call it the "Prayer of Rest." There are three well-established practices we can follow that are designed to lead us into the Prayer of Rest: solitude, silence, and recollection.

Many people try to avoid solitude because they are afraid of being alone. It may be that they have discovered that when they are alone and quiet, their innermost doubts and fears suddenly rush screaming to the surface. They may be bothered by a guilty conscience that rises up to condemn them when they are alone. Their solitude may amplify their awareness of being apart from God or of the emptiness of their lives. Whatever the reason, they find solitude distinctly uncomfortable.

I believe that we in the Church need to rediscover the spiritual benefits of solitude. Deliberately spending time alone for the purpose of meeting God is not only healthy for our souls, it is also biblical. Jesus taught solitude by both example and command.

> *And in the morning, a great while before day, he rose and went out to a lonely place, and there he prayed.*[15]

In his book *A Center of Quiet: Hearing God When Life Is Noisy*, Anglican priest David Runcorn states:

> He (Jesus) made silence and solitude His special companions. Whatever the demands upon Him, He always found a time and a place to hide away and be alone. His hectic teaching and ministering was constantly punctuated by these times of withdrawal. Before all the most important events in His life, we find Him preparing by getting alone. His ministry began in the wilderness (Mt. 4:1-11). He chose His disciples after a whole night alone in prayer (Lk. 6:12). When John the Baptist died, Jesus spent time alone (Mt.

14:13). Before the glory of the transfiguration and darkness of the Cross, we find Him alone in prayer (Mt. 17:1-9; 26:36-46). In those lonely places, the deep springs of the Spirit's life revived Him, the Father's will strengthened Him, and the Father's love inspired Him.

He taught the disciples to do the same. After one particular busy time of ministering and teaching He said, "'Come with Me by yourselves to a quiet place and get some rest.' So they went away by themselves in a boat to a solitary place" (Mk. 6:31-32).[16]

We All Need Time Alone With God

Jesus also promoted solitude by command.

But you, when you pray, go into your inner room, close your door and pray to your Father who is in secret, and your Father who sees what is done in secret will reward you.[17]

You will remember from Chapter Four that the "Father's house" is within us, and it has "many rooms." The more we retreat to our "inner room" to commune with our Lord, the more "rooms" we will discover within our heart that can contain prayer burdens that He gives us. My wife learned this a few years ago. One day the Holy Spirit was moving upon her in a very strong way and she felt so full that she thought she could not take any more. Then, the Lord began asking her questions: "Can you take more for Germany? Can you take more for Albania? Can you take more? Can you take more?" At each question, she looked deep within her heart and discovered another "room" that she didn't even know existed. She found that yes, she *could* take more. The Lord then filled those "rooms" with a portion of His heart—a burden for the people of those nations.

The point I am making is simply that the more time we spend praying in our "inner room," the more our capacity for prayer will grow. The more of ourselves we yield to the Lord in prayer, the more of His heart He can entrust us with.

Solitude helps us center our hearts on God. Dallas Willard, in his book *The Spirit of the Disciplines*, writes,

We must re-emphasize, the "desert" or "closet" is the primary place of strength for the beginner, as it was for Christ and for Paul. They show us by their example what we must do. In stark aloneness, it is possible to have silence, to be still and to know that Jehovah, indeed, is God (Ps. 46:10), to set the Lord before our minds with sufficient intensity and duration that we stay centered upon Him—our hearts fixed, established in trust (Ps. 112:7-8) even when back in the office, shop, or home.[18]

Some time back, I spent three days in solitude at a Francis of Assisi retreat center. I didn't speak to anyone the entire time; that was the whole point. (Besides, there wasn't anyone there that I knew anyway.) My favorite spot was a prayer room that had been dug out of the ground by hand. It was like a huge cavern, and was used as a place of solitude and silence, where a person could go to seek the Lord. The only available light was from a candle or a couple of small spotlights. I had some blessed hours with God there. It was so peaceful and tranquil. As I spent many hours there cut off from the distractions of the world, I found such a life of the Kingdom of God welling up within me. I let go and just let the Spirit feed my soul. It was wonderful.

Francois Fenelon, a 17th century French prelate and author, in his book *The Seeking Heart,* describes the benefits and rewards of solitary time with God.

> If you give up all those things that provoke your curiosity and set your mind spinning, you will have more than enough time to spend with God and to attend to your business. Living your life prayerfully will make you clear-headed and calm, no matter what happens. Your self-nature is overactive, impulsive, and always striving for something just outside your reach.
>
> But God, working within your spirit, produces a calm and faithful heart that the world cannot touch. I really want you to take an adequate amount of time to spend with God so that you might refresh your spirit. All your busyness surely drains you. Jesus took His disciples aside to be alone, and interrupted their most urgent business. Sometimes He would even leave people who had come from afar to see Him in order to come to His Father. I suggest you do the same. It is not enough to give out—you must learn to receive from God, too.[19]

Why then, is solitude so important? I have heard it stated very succinctly: "Come apart or *come apart.*"

Silence Is Golden

A second time-honored practice for entering the Prayer of Rest is silence, or the stilling within ourselves of what others have called the "creaturely activity."

To this end, Dallas Willard offers some practical advice:

> Hearing is said to be the last of our senses to go at death. Sound always strikes deeply and disturbingly into our souls. So, for the sake of our souls, we must seek times to leave our television, radio, tape players and telephones off. We should close off street noises as much as possible. We should try to find how quiet we can make our world by making whatever arrangements are necessary.[20]

It is said that Susannah Wesley, mother of John and Charles Wesley (and seventeen other children, eight of whom died in infancy), taught her children to leave her alone whenever they saw her with her apron over her head; it was her place of prayer. As I said before, one of my favorite places is sitting with a blanket over my head. I want to encourage you to find your own special place of prayer—a certain room or favorite chair perhaps—any place where you can get away and be silent before God. Today where we live in the beautiful hills of Williamson County, we have a "prayer gazebo" at the top peak of our land. There I sneak away, get a snapshot view of creation, and then in quietness commune with the Creator.

David Runcorn writes:

> If you have a magazine or newspaper handy, try reading an article without the punctuation marks. It doesn't make much sense, does it? It all becomes a hectic string of words. The meaning is lost. It lacks direction. The purpose of punctuation in a piece of writing is to guide the reader into the true meaning of the words and phrases; through it we understand. Punctuation also gives life and purpose to the words. Next time you see your favorite actor or actress on television, notice how cleverly they use timing—pauses and spaces—to give the words their meaning and power.
>
> Punctuation is a helpful way of thinking about Jesus' relationship with silence and solitude. His times alone were the commas, pauses, and full stops in the story of His life. They gave the rest of His life its structure, direction and balance.

His words and His works were born out of those hours of silent waiting upon God.[21]

Richard Foster, writing in the masterful book *Prayer: Finding the Heart's True Home*, accurately says:

This means not so much a silence of words as a silence of our grasping, manipulative control of people and situations. It means standing firm against our codependency drives to control everyone and fix everything.

This agitated creaturely activity hinders the work of God in us. In *silencio*, therefore, we still every motion that is not rooted in God. We become quiet, hushed, motionless, until we are finally centered... We let go of all distractions until we are driven into the Core. We allow God to reshuffle our priorities and eliminate unnecessary froth.[22]

Our Goal Is Greater Union With Christ

The third step for entering the Prayer of Rest is recollection, which we discussed in Chapter Three. It means coming into tranquillity of mind, heart, and spirit, with all in the proper balance. The prayer of rest is the place where growth and healing can take place.

What is our goal when we enter the Prayer of Rest? What are we after? We are seeking nothing less than greater union with Christ. I know this has been stated several times already, but that is because it is so fundamental to everything we are talking about here. Our goal in contemplative prayer is to enter into greater union with Christ and experience ever-increasing levels of spiritual intimacy with Him.

Juliana of Norwich, a 14th century English mystic, said, "The whole reason why we pray is to be united into the vision and contemplation of Him to whom we pray." Bonaventure, who was a follower of St. Francis of Assisi, stated, "Our final goal is union with God, which is a pure relationship where we see nothing."

From my own experience in trying to learn more of these overlooked contemplative ways, I discovered that as I began to quiet my soul before the Lord, I had to learn first how to bring the strongholds of my mind into captivity to Christ Jesus, and bring every thought into obedience to Him. That took awhile; it was a difficult struggle for me. Afterwards, though, I passed through the stage of recollection and entered into the place of communion with Him.

This is the place that is also sometimes called "listening prayer." It is the place where you can begin to hear the Lord and see into the realm of the Holy Spirit. Many times while in this reflective mood, I have activated for me the gift of discerning of spirits. In this room, I sometimes see lights flashing, almost like a display of colors coming forth. It is somewhat similar in my mind to the description in the Book of Revelation of the rainbow surrounding the throne of God. When I see these things, I realize they can represent the presence of God Himself. I am coming before Him!

It would be so easy just to stay in that place, a room of gifted-ness, and of seeing with spiritual eyes and hearing with spiritual ears. As wonderful as that room is, there is a room that is even better. There is a room that is deeper even than giftedness, and that is the place of fellowship with God Himself. In that place, nothing needs to be said. It is the "center of quiet"—the place where God is. More than just a room of gifts, it is the room of the Gift-giver Himself! That's why it is so much better. We could stay in the room of gifts, but Christ is calling us deeper. I don't know about you, but I want to press on! My soul waits for God and God alone. I want nothing less than union with Him in that center of quiet—where no words are spoken and no sound is heard—where He and I commune in silence together, Friend to friend, in an intimacy that is too deep and too precious for words.

Wisdom for the Journey

Our old friend Madame Guyon has some words of wisdom for us regarding our union with Christ.

As you come into the deeper level of knowing the Lord, you will eventually come to discover a principle I will call the law of central tendency.

As you continue holding your soul deep in your inward parts, you will discover that God has a magnetic attracting quality. Your God is like a magnet! The Lord naturally draws you more and more toward Himself.

We come now to the ultimate stage of Christian experience, Divine Union. This cannot be brought about merely by your own experience. Meditation will not bring Divine Union; neither will love, nor worship, nor your direction, nor your sacrifice…Eventually it will take an Act of God to make Union a reality.

Then let us agree on this: there is Divine Union, and there is a way. The way has a beginning, a progress and a point of arrival. Furthermore, the closer you come to the consum-mation, the more you put aside the things that helped you get started.

Of course, there is also a middle, for you cannot go from a beginning to an end without there being an intermediate space. But if the end is good and holy and necessary, and if the entrance is also good, you can be sure the journey between those two points is also good![23]

Indeed, it is a good journey, and a worthy one. Once the Lord has patiently and lovingly drawn us into the center of quiet with Him, we can rest in Him and enjoy His presence. At the same time we can reflect on the greatness of our God and His precious promises, and ponder in our heart His mighty ways.

Prayer for Quiet

In his book *Prayers From the Heart*, Richard Foster offers a "Prayer For Quiet," that I think is appropriate as a concluding thought because it speaks so pointedly to where most of us live.

I have, O Lord, a noisy heart. And entering outward silence doesn't stop the inner clamor. In fact, it seems only to make it worse. When I am full of activity, the internal noise is only a distant rumble; but when I get still, the rumble amplifies itself. And it is not like the majestic sound of a symphony rising to a grand crescendo; rather, it is the deafening din of clashing pots and clanging pans. What a racket! Worst of all, I feel helpless to hush the interior pandemonium.

Dear Lord Jesus, once you spoke peace to the wind and the waves. Speak Your shalom over my heart. I wait silently...patiently. I receive into the very core of my being Your loving command, "Peace, be still." Amen.[24]

Reflection Questions

1. What is at the center of a hurricane?
2. What historic Protestant group emphasized "centering" as part of their theology?
3. How can you maintain your peace in the midst of the storms of life?

Recommended Reading
The Center of Quiet by David Runcorn (InterVarsity Press, 1990)
Listening Prayer by Mary Ruth Swope (Whitaker, 1987)
Secret Prayer by Pat Gastineau (Word of Love Ministries, 1998)

Endnotes

1. Mark and Patti Virkler, *Communion with God*, Shippensburg, PA: Destiny Image Publishers, Inc., 1990, p. 49.
2. The discussion of all five ingredients of meditation in this section is adapted from Virkler, *Communion with God*, pp. 49-52.
3. Heb. 4:9-11.
4. Heb. 3:18-19.
5. Heb. 12:1-2.
6. Jn. 5:19.
7. Ps. 46:10.
8. Phil. 4:6-7.
9. Jn. 15:4-5.
10. Jn. 7:38-39a.
11. Virkler, *Communion with God*, p.54.
12. *Ibid*.
13. Jn. 15:15.
14. Virkler, *Communion with God*, p. 55.
15. Mk. 1:35 RSV.
16. David Runcorn, *A Center of Quiet: Hearing God When Life is Noisy*, Downers Grove, IL: InterVarsity Press, 1990, pp. 4,5.
17. Mt. 6:6.
18. Dallas Willard, *The Spirit of the Disciplines: Understanding How God Changes Lives*, New York, NY: Harper San Francisco, A Division of Harper Collins Publishers, 1991, pp. 62.
19. Francois Fenelon, *The Seeking Heart*, Sargent, GA: Christian Books Publishing House, 1962, p. 113.
20. Willard, *The Spirit of the Disciplines*, p. 63.
21. Runcorn, *A Center of Quiet*. p. 5.
22. Richard L. Foster, *Prayer: Finding the Heart's True Home*, New York, NY: Harper San Francisco, A Division of Harper Collins Publishers, Inc., 1992, p. 101.
23. Madame Jean Guyon, *Experiencing the Depths of Jesus Christ*, Sargent, GA; Christian Books Publishing House, 1962, p. 53.
24. Richard L. Foster, *Prayers From the Heart*, London, England: Hodder and Stoughton, 1996, p. 59.

Chapter Seven

Reflecting on the God Who Promises

As I explore the world of Christian mystical literature and plumb the depths of the Christian contemplative arts, I often feel like an archaeologist who has just unearthed a long-vanished and priceless artifact, or a diamond prospector who has just dug up a gem of singular beauty and purity. Each one I find makes me even more eager to keep digging for the next one, knowing that the treasure trove I have discovered is rich indeed, and practically inexhaustible.

One "gem" that is particularly precious to me is the spiritual discipline called meditation, or Christian meditative prayer. All but buried in the dust of history, it is virtually a lost art among believers today. One of the points I have been trying to make throughout this book is how important meditation and the other contemplative arts are to the Church *today*, and how I believe God wants to restore the practices on a wide-scale basis among His people. The best way to learn is to listen to the words of both modern and past masters.

Meditation Is a Gem With Many Facets

Meditation is not easy to define or explain. Like a diamond or other precious gem, it is best appreciated by examining it from different facets or angles. Basically, the word *meditate* means to "think deeply," or to "reflect on" something. To *reflect on* something means to "contemplate" or "ponder" it. *Contemplate* means to "gaze at or think about intensely." These words barely scratch the surface of what it means to meditate. Sometimes we will see something from one angle that we don't see from another, and which helps us understand. That's why I think that the best way to understand meditation (short of actually *doing* it) is to examine what several "experts" say about it—people who live the meditative life and know it by experience.

Elmer L. Towns, the vice president of Liberty University, has written a phenomenal book on the subject, called *Christian Meditation for Spiritual Breakthrough*. I have been prospecting in this particularly rich mine for some time now, and the great words of wisdom he shares come from someone who obviously is not an "armchair theologian," but who speaks out of his own personal experience. Here is what he says about Christian meditation:

> Christian meditation is not about what methods you use, nor is it about what position you assume, nor is it about what you chant or how you focus. Christian meditation is about God. It is meditation that will change your life because you focus on God—and when you experience God, God changes you.[1]

What Towns is saying is that, unlike other forms of meditation, Christian meditation does not focus on a method or a mantra or a posture, but on a *Person*—the living God. When our meditation brings us face-to-face with God, we cannot help but be changed.

Richard Foster, the author and Quaker teacher we met in earlier chapters, shares this insight:

> Throughout history all the devotional masters have viewed the meditative *scripturarum*—the meditation upon Scripture—as the central reference point by which all other forms of meditation are kept in proper perspective. In Meditative Prayer the Bible ceases to be a quotation dictionary, and becomes instead "wonderful words of life" that lead us to the Word of Life. It differs even from study of Scripture. Whereas the study of scripture centers upon exegesis, the meditation upon Scriptures centers on internalizing and personalizing the passage. The written Word becomes a living word addressed to us.[2]

The Need to Personalize and Internalize

One reason the Scriptures seem to lack life for so many believers is because they don't take the time to "internalize" and "personalize" what they read. Their hearts are not conditioned to hear the Lord speak to them.

Writing in *Meditating as a Christian*, author Peter Toon says,

Meditation is…thinking about, reflecting upon, considering, taking to heart, reading slowly and carefully, prayerfully taking in, and humbly receiving into mind, heart and will that which God has revealed. For Christian Meditation is being guided and inspired by the indwelling Spirit of Christ in the consideration of God's revelation.[3]

Christian meditation, then, focuses on God's revelation and depends on His Spirit for understanding.

Dietrich Bonhoeffer, the German pastor and theologian who was executed by the Nazis in 1945, compares meditation to the way we receive words from someone we love.

Just as you do not analyze the assets of someone you love, but accept them as they are said to you, then accept the Word of Scripture and ponder it in your heart, as Mary did. That is all. That is meditation.[4]

Bonhoeffer is talking here of more than just listening to words with the mind; he is speaking of listening with the *heart*. If we could all learn to practice this in all our relationships—listening to each with our hearts and not just our minds—what a dramatic difference it would make!

Dr. Sam Storms, the former director of the Grace Training Center in Kansas City, and now instructor at Wheaton College, sees meditation as a key to the spiritual renewing of our minds.

Meditation, then, is being attentive to God. It is a conscious, continuous engagement of the mind with God. This renewing of the mind (Rom. 12:1-2) is part of the process by which the Word of God penetrates the soul and spirit with the light of illumination and the power of transformation.[5]

In her marvelous book *The Soul at Rest*, Tricia McCary Rhodes describes meditative prayer using a gardening metaphor.

In meditative prayer the Bible is not a rulebook, a history lesson, or a treatise to be dissected and analyzed. We come to its author with our hearts open and our desire for Him.

We can hide God's Word in our hearts through meditative prayer. Seeking God's face, we want to understand the person who wrote these powerful words. Our hearts are the soil in which the Word is planted. Every part of our being joins together to nourish the seeds of truth until they sprout and bring life to our soul.[6]

Pat Gastineau, prayer leader for Word of Love Ministries, is a personal friend who my wife and I regard as a mentor in the areas of prayer and intercession. She has written a number of booklets on different aspects of the Christian's prayer life. Pat is a woman who lives what she writes. Here are some of her thoughts on Christian meditation.

Since meditation is mainly for the mind and the will, any meditation that is centered on Christ will hold the mind in place of loving attention toward God. Meditation can cause the mind to hold ideas and thoughts. As one centers his attention on certain aspects of God, the mind is being trained to focus for periods of time. Meditation brings discipline and therefore is one of the answers for unruly minds that tend to run loose. The Scriptures refer to the saving of the soul—the mind must be reprogramed to think correctly. Meditation will aid in producing a sound mind, one that is sane and sober.[7]

According to J. Adams, the author of *Ready to Restore* and many other Christian counseling materials, meditation seeks to apply the Word of God to daily life and circumstances.

Meditation is pondering over Scripture verses or passages in such a way that the written Word of God becomes a living Word of God, applied to our hearts by the Holy Spirit. The two primary words for meditation in the Bible mean "to murmur or mutter" and "to speak to one's self." Meditation is a process of thinking through language that takes place in the heart or inner life. The truth being meditated upon moves from mouth (murmuring), to the mind (reflective thinking), and finally to the heart (outer action). The person meditating seeks to understand how to relate Bible truth to life.[8]

We Need to Learn a Lesson From the Cow

Adams defines *meditation* with words like "pondering," "thinking through," "murmuring," and "reflective thinking." All of these terms suggest a careful, thoughtful process of analyzing the Word of God—"chewing" on it, if you will. When we meditate, we "chew" on God's Word until it is thoroughly digested. Then it can nourish our souls. I think that one of the best illustrations of this is to consider the digestive processes of a cow.

Cows are ruminants, meaning they chew the cud. If you know anything about cows, you know that they have more than one chamber in their stomach. Have you ever seen an old cow chewing? It's like somebody with a wad of bubblegum in his mouth; they just keep working it, and working it, and working it, until finally they swallow it. Then it comes back up and they chew on it some more, and chew on it, and chew on it, and finally, swallow it again. This process is called "ruminating."

In fact, the word *ruminate* means not only to "chew the cud," but also "to go over in the mind repeatedly and often casually or slowly," and "to engage in contemplation."[9] In his book *Prayer: Finding the Heart's True Home*, Richard Foster explains the analogy between a cow's digestive processes and Christian meditation.

> Have you ever watched a cow chew its cud? This unassuming animal will fill its stomach with grass and other food. Then it settles down quietly and, through a process of regurgitation, reworks what it has received, slowly moving its mouth in the process. In this way it is able to fully assimilate what it has previously consumed, which is then transformed into rich, creamy milk.
>
> So it is with Meditative Prayer. The truth being meditated upon passes from the mouth into the mind and down into the heart, where through quiet rumination—regurgitation, if you will—it produces in the person praying a loving, faith-filled response.[10]

It's How You Chew It

With meditation on Scripture it isn't so much a matter of how *much* you read as what you *chew* on. It may be no more than a single verse, or even just a part of a verse. It may be only a few words, such as "beside quiet waters." That's a phrase that the Lord had me chewing on for a long time. I thought about it, pondered it, and mused over it for months.

My mother says I was one of the most curious kids probably that ever was born, because I was always asking questions. To a certain degree I'm still that way. But now I ask God the questions, not, I hope, out of confusion or unbelief, but out of wonder and an insatiable curiosity. *What does this mean? Hmmm, let's try this angle on it.* Do you know what I mean? That's a form of meditation.

In the Book of Acts, when the apostles gave instructions to the church in Jerusalem to select servants, or deacons, to care for the widows and oversee the daily distribution of food, they gave as their reason

> *It is not desirable for us to neglect the word of God in order to serve tables. Therefore, brethren, select from among you seven men of good reputation, full of the Spirit and of wisdom, whom we may put in charge of this task. But we will devote ourselves to prayer and to the ministry of the word.*[11]

Note the order here. The apostles would devote themselves "to *prayer* and to the *ministry of the word.*" It isn't the other way around. It's not the ministry of the Word and prayer; it's prayer and the ministry of the Word. My point is this: prayer bathes the Word of God, and then the Word of God releases revelation into our lives. That's how we should approach God's Word, and that's what Christian meditative prayer is all about. It is a way of approaching the Word of God.

From Joshua We Can Learn to Meditate on the Promises of God

There are many different ways to approach or practice Christian meditation. Each of us must search out the way or ways that work best for us. What works for me may not work for you, and vice-versa. We are each "wired" differently, and we must find the way to pray, meditate, and worship that best connects with our personality and makeup and which is the most effective in helping to draw us into the presence of God.

In *Christian Meditation for Spiritual Breakthrough*, Elmer Towns presents ten different meditation models based on ten different personalities in the Bible. We cannot discuss them all here, but a brief description of a few will give you the idea. For example, there is "The Mary Model: Pondering the Person of Jesus." We will look at this model more closely in the next chapter. Then, there is "The Saint Paul Model: Becoming Like Christ," which we will discuss in Chapter Ten. In *this* chapter, I want to look at a model for meditation based on the life of Joshua, the successor of Moses.

Elmer Towns calls this "The Joshua Model: Focusing on Biblical Principles."[12] He writes:

> Those who follow the Joshua Model of meditation muse on
> the promises and principles of God's Word to bring them

God's success. "*This book of the Law shall not depart from your mouth, but you shall meditate in it day and night, that you may observe to do according to all that is written in it. For then you will make your way prosperous, and then you will have good success.*" (Josh. 1:8)

Joshua chewed on the words given to him by God through Moses and thus he found success. Should we not learn this art of meditation of focusing on Biblical principles, and also bear much fruit?[13]

Joshua's Faith in God Prepared Him for Success

Even a brief overview of what the Scriptures tell us about Joshua reveals a picture of a man whose whole life was a progression toward greater fellowship, intimacy, and union with God. The very first mention of Joshua in the Bible shows him as a servant and aide to Moses, the "friend"[14] of God. "So Moses said to Joshua, 'Choose men for us and go out, fight against Amalek...' Joshua did as Moses told him, and fought against Amalek..."[15] The Lord gave Joshua great victory in the battle. Apparently, at this early stage in Joshua's career, any word to Joshua from the Lord came through Moses; Joshua's direct communion with the Almighty lay in the future. "Then the Lord said to Moses, 'Write this in a book as a memorial and *recite it to Joshua*, that I will utterly blot out the memory of Amalek from under heaven'" (emphasis added).[16]

The next time we see Joshua, he is accompanying Moses to the "mountain of God." "So Moses arose with Joshua his servant, and Moses went up to the mountain of God."[17] Although Moses and Joshua went to the mountain together, only Moses entered the cloud of God's presence and glory, where he spent 40 days and nights in communion with the Lord and receiving the Law.

A Minister of the Presence

It seems that each time Joshua appears, his faith in and zeal for the Lord have grown and matured since the last time. The Bible gives us a clue to Joshua's increasing faith shortly after he and Moses came down from the mountain during the time of the Israelites' great sin with the golden calf. "Thus the Lord used to speak to Moses face to face, just as a man speaks to his friend. When Moses returned to the camp, his servant Joshua, the son of Nun, a young man, would not depart from the tent."[18] Joshua was a servant in the sense of performing spiritual service. The word also means "minister." Although

Joshua was not strictly a "young man" in terms of years (he was probably about 50 years old), the term "young man" was commonly applied to those who performed spiritual service.

The clearest clue to his deepening commitment, however, is that "Joshua...would not depart from the tent." This tent was most likely a special place that had been set up for worshiping the Lord. Although the King James Version uses the word "tabernacle" here, the tabernacle of Moses, for which God gave instructions on the mountain, had not yet been built. The point is, Joshua was in the place of worship and spiritual service and *would not leave it*. Joshua may not have been aware of it at the time, but he was being groomed to succeed Moses as the leader of Israel.

Joshua's life consistently displayed his faith and loyalty to God. He was one of the 12 spies chosen by Moses to reconnoiter the land of Canaan (Num. 13:16), and one of only two (Caleb was the other) who brought back a favorable and encouraging report. When the people of Israel refused to obey the Lord and enter the land, Joshua was grief-stricken.

> *Joshua the son of Nun and Caleb the son of Jephunneh, of those who had spied out the land, tore their clothes; and they spoke to all the congregation of the sons of Israel, saying, "The land which we passed through to spy out is an exceedingly good land. If the Lord is pleased with us, then He will bring us into this land and give it to us—a land which flows with milk and honey. Only do not rebel against the Lord; and do not fear the people of the land, for they will be our prey. Their protection has been removed from them, and the Lord is with us; do not fear them."*[19]

The Graduation Through Faithfulness

Because of Joshua's faithfulness, God promised that he would indeed enter the land of Canaan. He and Caleb, alone of that entire generation of Israelites 20 years old and older, would live to enter the land (Num. 14:30). All of the others, because of their unbelief and rebellion, would die in the wilderness over the next 40 years.

As the time for the transfer of leadership approached, the preparation of Joshua intensified. He was publicly anointed as Moses' successor.

> *So the Lord said to Moses, "Take Joshua the son of Nun, a man in whom is the Spirit, and lay your hand on him; and have him stand before Eleazar the priest and before all the congregation,*

and commission him in their sight. You shall put some of your authority on him, in order that all the congregation of the sons of Israel may obey him"... Moses did just as the Lord commanded him...[20]

Joshua received words of instruction and encouragement from the Lord.

Then the Lord said to Moses, "Behold, the time for you to die is near; call Joshua, and present yourselves at the tent of meeting, that I may commission him." So Moses and Joshua went and presented themselves at the tent of meeting. The Lord appeared in the tent in a pillar of cloud, and the pillar of cloud stood at the doorway of the tent...Then He commissioned Joshua the son of Nun, and said, "Be strong and courageous, for you shall bring the sons of Israel into the land which I swore to them, and I will be with you."[21]

This is the first recorded instance of the Lord speaking *directly* to Joshua, but Moses is present. The transfer is not yet complete. But what a promise! "I will be with you." I can't help but wonder what kind of communion with God Joshua had been enjoying all these years during his *private* times of worship!

Joshua's Obedience to God Guaranteed His Success

With the death of Moses, the transfer of leadership was complete. "Now Joshua the son of Nun was filled with the spirit of wisdom, for Moses had laid his hands on him; and the sons of Israel listened to him and did as the Lord had commanded Moses."[22] Joshua had spent most of his life in preparation for this moment. Through a lifetime of faithfulness, worship, and communion with the Lord, Joshua was prepared for success in leading the nation of Israel into the Promised Land. It was now, at last, that the Lord spoke to Joshua *directly* for the first time without Moses present. By virtue of his position and because of the growth in his intimate relationship with God, Joshua was favored from here on with direct word from the Lord.

Listen to the promises God gave Joshua, and consider His instructions to the new leader.

Now it came about after the death of Moses the servant of the Lord, that the Lord spoke to Joshua the son of Nun, Moses' servant, saying, "Moses My servant is dead; now therefore arise, cross this Jordan, you and all this people, to the land which I am giving to them, to the sons of Israel. Every place on which the sole of your foot treads, I have given it to you, just as I spoke to Moses. From the wilderness and this Lebanon, even as far as the great river, the river Euphrates, all the land of the Hittites, and as far as the Great Sea toward the setting of the sun will be your territory. No man will be able to stand before you all the days of your life. Just as I have been with Moses, I will be with you; I will not fail you or forsake you. Be strong and courageous, for you shall give this people possession of the land which I swore to their fathers to give them. Only be strong and very courageous; be careful to do according to all the law which Moses My servant commanded you; do not turn from it to the right or to the left, so that you may have success wherever you go. This book of the law shall not depart from your mouth, but you shall meditate on it day and night, so that you may be careful to do according to all that is written in it; for then you will make your way prosperous, and then you will have success. Have I not commanded you? Be strong and courageous! Do not tremble or be dismayed, for the Lord your God is with you wherever you go."[23]

The Commission Given—Meditate on My Word

The Lord promised His presence and His power to be with Joshua wherever he went: "I will be with you; I will not fail you or forsake you." What a promise! No enemy would stand and no obstacle would defeat Joshua and the Israelites as they entered Canaan to take the land. The Lord would give them victory, just as He had promised Moses. Now He was giving the promise to Joshua. The condition was absolute obedience: "...be careful to do according to all the law which Moses My servant commanded you; do not turn from it to the right or to the left, so that you may have success wherever you go." This is why the Lord could encourage Joshua three times to "be strong and courageous."

Then notice what the Lord says in verse 8: "This book of the law shall not depart from your mouth, but you shall meditate on it day and night, so that you may be careful to do according to all that is written in it; for then you will make your way prosperous, and then you will have success." I think it is significant that God issues three basic commands to Joshua: be strong and courageous, be obedient, and *meditate on My Word*.

It was not to "depart" from his mouth. Joshua was to "chew" on the Word of the Lord day and night, murmuring and muttering it, working it over and over like a cow chewing its cud, ruminating and pondering it. He was to speak it into his heart and soul—to be possessed by the Word of God. In this way, Joshua would *know* and *understand* the Lord's commands—both prerequisites for obedience. We can't obey the Word of the Lord if we do not *know* the Word of the Lord.

The entire Book of Joshua is a record of Joshua's faithful and careful obedience to the God who had called him, prepared him, and shaped him—the God he had grown to love with all his heart. As a result, God fulfilled His promises. Joshua experienced success and victory wherever he went. At the same time, Joshua grew closer to the heart of the God he loved. For only one example, consider the following:

In order to help Israel honor a treaty and defeat their enemies in a great battle, God performed a great miracle at Joshua's request, thus fulfilling His promises to always be with him, to never fail or forsake him, and to give him success.

> *Then Joshua spoke to the Lord in the day when the Lord delivered up the Amorites before the sons of Israel, and he said in the sight of Israel, "O sun, stand still at Gibeon, and O moon in the valley of Aijalon." So the sun stood still, and the moon stopped, until the nation avenged themselves of their enemies. Is it not written in the book of Jashar? And the sun stopped in the middle of the sky, and did not hasten to go down for about a whole day. And there was no day like that before it or after it, when the Lord listened to the voice of a man; for the Lord fought for Israel.*[24]

When God Listens to the Voice of a Man

Why did God "listen to the voice" of Joshua? First, it was to honor His name and His promises. Second, it was to honor a man who had been whole-hearted in his obedience and pure-hearted in his love. Only someone in intimate fellowship and union with God could have the boldness and confidence to make such a request of God! Joshua did, and God answered!

In the final analysis, what was the testimony of Joshua's life? I think it can be summed up in three statements, one by Joshua, and two made of him by others.

1. Joshua was *complete* in his obedience: "Just as the Lord had commanded Moses his servant, so Moses commanded

Joshua, and so Joshua did; he left nothing undone of all that the Lord had commanded Moses."[25]

2. Joshua was *completely devoted* to God: "...as for me and my house, we will serve the Lord."[26]

3. Joshua *influenced the nation for good* as long as he lived: "Israel served the Lord all the days of Joshua and all the days of the elders who survived Joshua, and had known all the deeds of the Lord which He had done for Israel."[27]

Joshua learned to meditate on the promises of God, but even more importantly, he learned how to meditate on the God of promises. That's the lesson of Joshua's life. Simply stated, the *goal*, the *purpose*, the *object*, and the *source* of our meditation is *God Himself*!

Reflection Questions

1. What is the goal of Christian meditative prayer?
2. What can you learn from the life of Joshua as it pertains to the art of meditation?
3. What are some practical steps necessary to cultivate meditative prayer?

Recommended Reading

Christian Meditation for Spiritual Breakthrough by Elmer Towns (Regal Books, 1999)

The Soul at Rest by Tricia McCary Rhodes (Bethany House Publishers, 1996)

Disciplines of the Holy Spirit by Dr. Siang-Yang Tan (Zondervan Publishing House, 1997)

Endnotes

1. Elmer L. Towns, *Christian Meditation for Spiritual Breakthrough*, Ventura, CA: Regal Books, 1999, p. 21.

2. Richard Foster, *Prayer: Finding the Heart's True Home*, San Francisco, CA: Harper Collins, 1992, p. 146.

3. Peter Toon, *Meditating as a Christian*, London: Collins Religious Department, part of Harper Collins Publishing, 1991, p. 61.

4. Dietrich Bonhoeffer, *The Way to Freedom*, New York: Harper and Row, 1966, p. 263.

5. Sam Storms, *Devotional Life Class Notes*, Grace Training Center, Kansas City, 1996.

6. Tricia McCary Rhodes, *The Soul at Rest*, Minneapolis, MN: Bethany House Publishers, 1996, pp. 53-54.

7. Pat Gastineau, *Contemplative Prayer*, Word of Love Ministries, 1999, pp. 8-9.

8. J. Adams, *Ready to Restore: The Layman's Guide to Christian Counseling*, Grand Rapids, MI: Baker, 1981, pp. 64,65

9. "ruminate," *Merriam-Webster's Collegiate Dictionary*, *Tenth edition*,

Springfield, MA: Merriam-Webster, Inc., 1996, p. 1024.

10. Foster, *Prayer: Finding the Heart's True Home*, p. 143.
11. Acts 6:2b-4.
12. Towns, *Christian Meditation for Spiritual Breakthrough*, pp. 29-31.
13. *Ibid.*
14. Ex. 33:11.
15. Ex. 17:9a, 10a.
16. Ex. 17:14.
17. Ex. 24:13.
18. Ex. 33:11.
19. Num. 14:6-10.
20. Num. 27:18-20, 22a.
21. Deut. 31:14-15, 23.
22. Deut. 34:9.
23. Josh. 1:1-9.
24. Josh. 10:12-14.
25. Josh. 11:15.
26. Josh. 24:15b.
27. Josh. 24:31.

Chapter Eight

The Ponderings of the Heart

Joshua loved the Lord with all his heart and served Him all the days of his life. Through worship, Joshua experienced the love of God; through obedience he experienced the presence and power of God. By reflecting on the God who promises, Joshua came to know God in an intimate and personal way. Worship, obedience, reflection; all of these are linked together. Each is a critical and indispensable part of knowing and walking with the Lord.

Reflection—thinking quietly and calmly with a specific focus— is one facet of meditation. Another closely related facet is pondering, which means to "weigh in the mind" and "to think or consider quietly, soberly, and deeply." It implies the "careful weighing of a problem" or a situation.[1] Joshua reflected on God. Since Jesus Christ was "God in the flesh," the New Testament equivalent would be to reflect on or to ponder the Person of Jesus. This is another powerful meditation model, and a perfect illustration is found in the life of Mary, the mother of Jesus.[2]

As we begin to look at the "Mary Model," the words of Elmer Towns can help focus and direct our thoughts:

Can you begin to imagine what Mary pondered on? Just think—the Son of God growing inside of you. You feel His heartbeat; you feel His foot move; you bring Him to birth! Truly, one of the closest people ever to Jesus was His mother, Mary. "Mary kept all these things and pondered them in her heart." (Lk. 2:19) She knew Him better than anyone, yet just like us, she wanted to know Him still better. Mary becomes our example of what it means to really know Christ—to come into intimacy with the lover of our soul. Let's join in her model of meditating upon the person of Christ Jesus.[3]

As a man, I cannot identify as fully with Mary in this regard as my wife can. However, I distinctly remember seeing that foot go across her protruding stomach and thinking, *That's Justin or Grace Ann,* or feeling that elbow pressing from beneath the skin, and being amazed and boasting, "That's Tyler or Rachel." I remember putting my ear to her belly to listen for whatever I could hear. Sometimes I even played classical music to inspire our unborn children. So even though I can't connect completely with Mary, I can connect to the extent of having experienced four live little miracles growing inside my wife, and in being present at their births.

Of course, being able to identify with Mary as a mother is not the only connection point for pondering the Person of Jesus Christ; it is only one of many points of departure. However, I believe there is much that we can learn from Mary's example that will help us in our own journey into the deeper life with Christ.

Mary Pondered God's Choice of Her to Bear His Son

Can you picture in your mind what it might have been like for Mary—a virgin who may have been as young as fifteen years of age—that day in Nazareth when she received an angelic visitor?

Now in the sixth month the angel Gabriel was sent from God to a city in Galilee called Nazareth, to a virgin engaged to a man whose name was Joseph, of the descendants of David; and the virgin's name was Mary. And coming in, he said to her, "Greetings, favored one! The Lord is with you." But she was very perplexed at this statement, and kept pondering what kind of salutation this was. The angel said to her, "Do not be afraid, Mary; for you have found favor with God. And behold, you will conceive in your womb and bear a son, and you shall name Him Jesus. He will be great and will be called the Son of the Most High; and the Lord God will give Him the throne of His father David; and He will reign over the house of Jacob forever, and His kingdom will have no end."[4]

What was going through Mary's mind at that moment? The text says that she was "perplexed" and "pondering," trying to understand what the angel meant. Gabriel set her heart and mind at ease with the words, "Do not be afraid." Reflect for a moment on his next words: "you have found favor with God." What an incredible, beautiful, and wonderful statement! Can there be any greater joy or any deeper wonder than to know that we enjoy God's *favor*? Not by anything we have done, it is an act of pure divine grace. The same was true with Mary. In His divine sovereignty, God *chose* to favor Mary. His favor was to entrust to her the incarnation of His only begotten Son! What an awesome privilege to bear the Son of God! What an awesome responsibility! Yet, God saw in Mary qualities of faith and character that He was looking for. This is revealed in Mary's response to Gabriel's announcement.

> *Mary said to the angel, "How can this be, since I am a virgin?"*
> *The angel answered and said to her, "The Holy Spirit will come*
> *upon you, and the power of the Most High will overshadow you;*
> *and for that reason the holy Child shall be called the Son of God.*
> *And behold, even your relative Elizabeth has also conceived a son*
> *in her old age; and she who was called barren is now in her sixth*
> *month. For nothing will be impossible with God." And Mary*
> *said, "Behold, the bondslave of the Lord; may it be done to me*
> *according to your word." And the angel departed from her.*[5]

Mary's question, "How can this be...?" is not a question of challenge or unbelief, but of awe and wonder. I don't think she doubted God's power; she just didn't know *how* He would accomplish it. She probably also wondered why God had chosen *her*. This is where her simple faith and humility shine through.

Once Gabriel has set Mary's spirit at peace and answered her question, her next statement reveals her heart and character. Mary doesn't preen with pride at being the Lord's "chosen." Rather, she says "Behold the *bondslave* of the Lord; may it be done to me according to your word." In other words, Mary was saying, "I belong to God; I live to do His bidding." This was not fatalistic resignation, but an expression of *willing and joyful obedience!*

Mary did not fully understand what was happening, but her heart belonged to the Lord. Whatever lay ahead, she trusted Him to be with her and to fulfill all that He had told her.

Mary Pondered the Work of Her Coming Son

After Gabriel's announcement, Mary had plenty of time to reflect on what she had been told and to ponder the significance of the child growing in her womb. During a visit to her cousin Elizabeth, who was pregnant with John the Baptist, Mary was caught up in an ecstasy of praise to God, in which her ponderings linked her coming son to the fulfillment of God's promises to Israel throughout many generations.

> *And Mary said: "My soul exalts the Lord, / And my spirit has rejoiced in God my Savior. / For He has had regard for the humble state of His bondslave; / For behold, from this time on all generations will count me blessed. / For the Mighty One has done great things for me; / And holy is His name. / And His mercy is upon generation after generation / Toward those who fear Him. / He has done mighty deeds with His arm; / He has scattered those who were proud in the thoughts of their heart. / He has brought down rulers from their thrones, / And has exalted those who were humble. / He has filled the hungry with good things; / And sent away the rich empty-handed. / He has given help to Israel His servant, / In remembrance of His mercy, / As He spoke to our fathers, / To Abraham and his descendants forever."* [6]

Mary was beginning to understand a little of the magnitude of God's plan. She recognized that the baby developing inside her was a continuation of God's age-old pattern of blessing, redemption, and promise fulfillment for His people. As for her own role in God's plan—the role for which He Himself had chosen her—Mary considered herself greatly blessed. Finally, after centuries of God's faithfulness to His people, He was giving "help to Israel His servant," and Mary was a part of it! She was willing to be "wasted on Jesus!"

Mary Pondered the Nature of Her Newborn Son

The events surrounding the birth of Jesus gave Mary another occasion to ponder the activity of God in her life and in the world. It would be hard to conceive humbler circumstances than those under which Jesus came: born to poor parents in a tiny, insignificant, "backwater" village so overcrowded because of the census that the only available place for the birth was a cave that was used as a stable. There was no fanfare, no party or big celebration to announce the birth of a King—at least, nothing from the hand of man.

At some point during the night, Mary and Joseph received some humble visitors—shepherds from the nearby fields—who told them an amazing story. They had been visited by an angel who had told them of "good news of great joy which will be for all the people; for today in the city of David there has been born for you a Savior, who is Christ the Lord." [7] The angel had told them the baby would be found in a manger. Then, an entire *army* of angels had appeared and proclaimed, "Glory to God in the highest, / And on earth peace among men with whom He is pleased."[8] After this announcement, the shepherds had wasted no time. In the words of Luke,

> *When the angels had gone away from them into heaven, the shepherds began saying to one another, "Let us go straight to Bethlehem then, and see this thing that has happened which the Lord has made known to us." So they came in a hurry and found their way to Mary and Joseph, and the baby as He lay in the manger. When they had seen this, they made known the statement which had been told them about this Child. And all who heard it wondered at the things which were told them by the shepherds. But Mary treasured all these things, pondering them in her heart.*[9]

What were the "things" that Mary "treasured" and "pondered" in her heart? First of all, it was the fact that the birth of her son was "good news of great joy...for all the people." I wonder what Mary thought of that in light of the quiet and unassuming conditions of the moment. Second, her son Jesus was the "Savior...Christ the Lord." At that time, did Mary have any idea, any inkling, that her son would have to die in order to fulfill His role as Savior? Third, Mary pondered the fact that the humble birth of her son was significant enough to warrant being heralded from Heaven by an angelic chorus. Did she wonder what it was going to be like to be the mother of the Son of God?

Mary Pondered the Destiny of Her Son

Jesus' first public miracle took place during a wedding feast, and Mary, His mother was there. In fact, in a way, she was the initiator.

> *On the third day there was a wedding in Cana of Galilee, and the mother of Jesus was there; and both Jesus and His disciples were invited to the wedding. When the wine ran out, the mother of Jesus said to Him, "They have no wine." And Jesus said to her, "Woman, what does that have to do with us? My hour has not yet come." His mother said to the servants, "Whatever He says to you, do it." Now there were six stone waterpots set there for the Jewish custom of purification, containing twenty or thirty gallons each. Jesus said to them, "Fill the waterpots with water." So they filled them up to the brim. And He said to them, "Draw some out now and take it to the headwaiter." So they took it to him. When the headwaiter tasted the water which had become wine, and did*

*not know where it came from (but the servants who had drawn the
water knew), the headwaiter called the bridegroom, and said to
him, "Every man serves the good wine first, and when the people
have drunk freely, then he serves the poorer wine; but you have
kept the good wine until now." This beginning of His signs Jesus
did in Cana of Galilee, and manifested His glory, and His disciples believed in Him.*[10]

When the wine ran out, why did Mary turn to her son Jesus for
a solution? As far as we know from the biblical record, she had not
yet seen Him perform any miracles. As Jesus Himself told her, His
"hour" had not yet come. Perhaps she looked to Him partly out of
habit. It is very possible that Joseph by this time was dead and Jesus,
as the eldest, was now the head of the home. Besides, she had had
thirty years to ponder her son's destiny, announced at His birth, as
well as to observe His uniquely sinless life.[11] What was it like to live
daily with a *sinless* son, who was respectful and obedient, who never
talked back, and who never did anything deserving rebuke or pun-
ishment? How did Mary feel being for thirty years continuously in
the company of the divine Son of God, watching Him grow from
helpless infancy, through awkward adolescence, into strong, mature,
and virile manhood?

For whatever reason, Mary obviously had confidence that Jesus
could do something about the wine situation. Jesus' response to her
was neither disrespectful nor a refusal. When He called her
"Woman," Jesus was using a term of affection and respect. "His question seeks to lead one to see the connection between the revelation of
His glory and the sign-miracle He was about to do. Mary's response
indicates that Jesus will do something about the discovered need."[12]

Years of pondering the Person of Jesus apparently had led Mary
to the conviction that her son had a unique destiny to fulfill and a singular mission to accomplish. Did she understand yet that it would
lead to His death?

Aside from meeting a genuine need in an embarrassing social
situation, Jesus' act of turning the water to wine was an announcement of His entry into His public ministry. It was in one sense a symbolic act. "Wine typically speaks of the joy of spiritual life. With the
coming of Jesus, God's best has arrived at last…Jesus turns water
into wine in joyful celebration of a new age."[13] Did Mary understand
this? Is that why she turned to Jesus when the wine ran out? Perhaps
her pondering led her to believe that her son's "hour" *had* arrived.

Mary Pondered the Death of Her Son

*How could it all end so soon? Was He born just so He could die so horribly? God, is **this** part of Your plan? How can it be?* No one knows what thoughts went through Mary's mind, what piercings of her heart, as she stood on Calvary and pondered Jesus as He hung on the cross. Did she comprehend at that moment that her beloved son was the Lamb of God who was to die to take away the sin of the world, or did that understanding come to her later? Did she rehearse in her mind all the promises and prophecies, and all the hopes and dreams she had stored up over the last 33 years? Did she try to add them all up to see if somehow they equaled crucifixion?

> *But standing by the cross of Jesus were His mother, and His mother's sister, Mary the wife of Clopas, and Mary Magdalene. When Jesus then saw His mother, and the disciple whom He loved standing nearby, He said to His mother, "Woman, behold, your son!" Then He said to the disciple, "Behold, your mother!" From that hour the disciple took her into his own household.*[14]

Whatever Mary's thoughts may have been, Jesus was thinking about her. As the probable head of the household, Jesus was responsible for His mother's welfare. Since He would no longer be able to be with her, He placed her in the care of John, "the disciple whom He loved." From that day forward, John looked on Mary as if she was his mother, and she looked on John as if he was her son. Why didn't Jesus put Mary under the care of one of His brothers? First of all, they apparently were not present. Second of all, at the time of Jesus' death, none of His brothers believed in Him as the Messiah. Jesus placed His mother, a believer, under the care of John, also a believer.

Mary's ponderings of the Person of Jesus on the cross taught her that the road to joy, fellowship, and full union with God inevitably leads through thickets of pain, sorrow, and anguish of heart.

Mary Pondered the Victory of Her Risen Son

Like Jesus' disciples and other followers, Mary probably did not expect to see her son again after He was removed from the cross and buried. Apparently, none of Jesus' followers expected Him to rise from the dead. The discovery of the empty tomb surprised them as much as it did anybody else. Only when Jesus appeared visibly and bodily to them did their doubts disappear. Although the New Testament does not specifically state that the risen Jesus appeared to His mother, Mary, I cannot accept the idea that He would not have shown

Himself to the one person on earth who was closer to Him than any other. In First Corinthians, Paul talks about the post-resurrection appearances of Jesus.

> *For I delivered to you as of first importance what I also received, that Christ died for our sins according to the Scriptures, and that He was buried, and that He was raised on the third day according to the Scriptures, and that He appeared to Cephas, then to the twelve. After that He appeared to more than five hundred brethren at one time, most of whom remain until now, but some have fallen asleep; then He appeared to James, then to all the apostles; and last of all, as to one untimely born, He appeared to me also.*[15]

Certainly, Mary was among this company! I believe Jesus' brothers were included, too. In fact, the "James" to whom Paul refers, who later became the leader of the Jerusalem church, was the half-brother of Jesus. Prior to the resurrection, there is no evidence that Jesus' brothers believed in Him as Lord and Savior. Afterwards, however, they are listed, along with Mary, among those who were in the "upper room" in Jerusalem, waiting for the coming of the Holy Spirit. What could have turned them around, other than seeing the risen Jesus in the flesh?

An Upper Room Experience

Just before His ascension, Jesus commanded His followers to remain in Jerusalem until the Holy Spirit came. Then, imbued with the power of the Spirit, they would carry the gospel message to the ends of the earth. Having said these things, Jesus departed into Heaven.

> *Then they returned to Jerusalem from the mount called Olivet, which is near Jerusalem, a Sabbath day's journey away. When they had entered the city, they went up to the upper room where they were staying; that is, Peter and John and James and Andrew, Philip and Thomas, Bartholomew and Matthew, James the son of Alphaeus, and Simon the Zealot, and Judas the son of James. These all with one mind were continually devoting themselves to prayer, along with the women, and Mary the mother of Jesus, and with His brothers.*[16]

What were Mary's thoughts as she prayed and waited with the others in that upper room? She had watched Jesus die; now she had seen Him alive again! As a child, Jesus had submitted to her authority as His mother; now she submitted to His authority as her Lord. Was it beginning to make sense to her? Did she now comprehend the breadth and the depth of God's eternal plan? On the Day of Pentecost, when the "tongue as of fire" rested upon her, and as the divine, holy Presence descended to dwell within her and bubbled up from her spirit, did Mary finally, fully understand who He was, this Jesus whom she had called "son," and now knew as "Lord"?

A lifetime of pondering the Person of Jesus had brought matchless treasure, wonder, and richness to Mary's spirit. As she had said so many years before, the Mighty One *had* done great things for her, and every generation *would* count her as *exceedingly* blessed!

Once We See Jesus As He Is, Nothing Else Matters

Pondering the Person of Jesus Christ helps us put all the rest of life into proper relationship, because once we see Jesus *as He really is,* our perspective changes forever. Three of Jesus' disciples discovered this vividly one day when they accompanied Jesus to the top of a mountain.

> *And Jesus was saying to them, "Truly I say to you, there are some of those who are standing here who will not taste death until they see the kingdom of God after it has come with power."*

> *Six days later, Jesus took with Him Peter and James and John, and brought them up on a high mountain by themselves. And He was transfigured before them; and His garments became radiant and exceedingly white, as no launderer on earth can whiten them. Elijah appeared to them along with Moses; and they were talking with Jesus. Peter said to Jesus, "Rabbi, it is good for us to be here; let us make three tabernacles, one for You, and one for Moses, and one for Elijah." For he did not know what to answer; for they became terrified. Then a cloud formed, overshadowing them, and a voice came out of the cloud, "This is My beloved Son, listen to Him!" All at once they looked around and saw no one with them anymore, except Jesus alone.*[17]

When Peter, James, and John went up the mountain with Jesus, He was "transfigured" before them. For a few mesmerizing moments the three disciples saw their Master as they had never seen Him before. They were allowed to catch a glimpse of His glory—the glory that was His as the Son of God. At the same time, the figures of Moses and Elijah appeared, and were talking with Jesus. How did the disciples recognize them as Moses and Elijah? I think, perhaps, that it was through divine revelation, although there may have been some visible clues.

Apart from their literal presence, I believe that the appearance of Moses and Elijah had symbolic meaning as well. Moses represented the Law; Elijah, the Prophets. For a devout Jew, the Law and the Prophets comprised the sum total of life. Jesus was the fulfillment and completion of both.

Awe-struck Peter was ready to camp out on the mountaintop. The passage says that the three disciples were "terrified," yet Peter also said, "it is good to be here." They were caught up in a "holy terror," an awesome fear and reverence that is known only to those who have found themselves in the Presence of the Almighty. Peter was a talker; he offered to build three tabernacles for the three exalted figures that stood before him. He might have found it easy to get caught up talking with Moses and Elijah about the past or present activity of God.

This, however, was not a time for *talking*; it was a time for *listening*. A cloud surrounded them and the voice of God spoke from within it: "This is My beloved Son, listen to Him!" At that moment, Peter, James, and John saw no one else with them—except Jesus. Moses and Elijah were gone. Certainly, the lawgiver and the prophet had literally disappeared from sight, but I believe there is symbolic meaning here as well. This Scripture depicts the jealousy of the Father for His Son and demonstrates His great longing to speak to us. In order to hear God, we must become so focused on Him that everything else fades into the background. In one sense, Peter, James, and John no longer saw Moses and Elijah because the Father directed their eyes to see Jesus *alone*. When we ponder the Person of Jesus, we are learning to focus our minds, our thoughts, and our hearts on Him to the exclusion of all else.

Once We See Jesus As He Is, Our "Seeing" Is Changed Forever

I'm sure Peter, James, and John never looked at Jesus the same way again after their experience on the mountain. Seeing Jesus as He truly was, revealed in His glory, changed their perspective forever. Unfortunately, no written record exists that states in his own words how the apostle James saw Jesus. He wrote no part of the New Testament and was the first of the apostles to die, being martyred by King Herod Agrippa around AD 44.

It is different with Peter and John, however. The New Testament has preserved some of their Spirit-inspired impressions and descriptions of Jesus, the fruit of years of contemplating, meditating, reflecting, and pondering His Person.

Here is how Peter saw Jesus:

- *God has made Him both Lord and Christ—this Jesus whom you crucified.*[18]

- *He is the stone which was rejected by you, the builders, but which became the chief corner stone. And there is salvation in no one else; for there is no other name under heaven that has been given among men by which we must be saved.*[19]

- *Christ also suffered for you, leaving you an example for you to follow in His steps, who committed no sin, nor was any deceit found in His mouth…and He Himself bore our sins in His body on the cross, so that we might die to sin and live to righteousness; for by His wounds you were healed.*[20]

- *For we did not follow cleverly devised tales when we made known to you the power and coming of our Lord Jesus Christ, but we were eyewitnesses of His majesty. For when He received honor and glory from God the Father, such an utterance as this was made to Him by the Majestic Glory, "This is My beloved Son with whom I am well-pleased"—and we ourselves heard this utterance made from heaven when we were with Him on the holy mountain.*[21]

In some ways, John's understanding of Jesus was even more profound than Peter's. This may be due partly to the fact that John wrote as much as sixty years after the death of Jesus—plenty of time for his ponderings to take full shape and form.

- *In the beginning was the Word, and the Word was with God, and the Word was God. He was in the beginning with God. All things came into being through Him, and apart from Him nothing came into being that has come into being. In Him was life, and the life was the Light of men…But as many as received Him, to them He gave the right to become children of God, even to those who believe in His name.*[22]

- *And the Word became flesh, and dwelt among us, and we saw His glory, glory as of the only begotten from the Father, full of grace and truth.*[23]

Pondering the Person of Jesus Christ is an important model of meditation for us because it is in pondering Jesus that we really begin to *know* Him as He reveals Himself to us. It is only in *knowing* Jesus that we can begin to become *like* Jesus, and becoming *Christ-like* is the purpose of our daily walk of faith.

Radical Transformation

Do you long for change? Do you want to go deeper with God? Ponderings of the Heart, then, is a recipe written just for you! As we meditate upon the wonders of this man Christ Jesus; as we reach upward and inward to the Lover of our soul; we become changed! This age old method sounds like another great means of becoming "wasted on Jesus." It will lead to radical transformation.

Yes, pursuing Christ-likeness leads us toward greater union with Him. The apostle Paul understood this, which is why he made that pursuit the focus of his life.

Reflection Questions

1. What things did Mary, the mother of Jesus, ponder in her heart?
2. What lessons can you learn from the life of Mary?
3. What things do you ponder in your heart and cherish the most?

Recommended Reading

Waiting on God by Andrew Murray (Whitaker, 1981)
Kneeling on the Promises by Jim W. Goll (Chosen Books, 1999)
The Way of the Heart by Henri Nouwen (Ballantine, 1983)

Endnotes

1. "ponder," *Merriam-Webster's Collegiate Dictionary, Tenth Edition*, Springfield, MA: Merriam-Webster, Inc., 1996, p. 905.
2. Elmer Towns, *Christian Meditation for Spiritual Breakthrough*, Ventura, CA: Regal Books, 1999, pp. 29-31.
3. *Ibid*.
4. Lk. 1:26-33.
5. Lk. 1:34-38.
6. Lk. 1:46-55.
7. Lk. 2:10b-11.
8. Lk. 2:14.
9. Lk. 2:15-19.
10. Jn. 2:1-11.
11. *New Commentary on the Whole Bible, New Testament Volume*, Based on the classic commentary of Jamieson, Fausset, and Brown; J. D. Douglas, gen. Ed., Philip W. Comfort, New Testament ed., (printed version) Wheaton, IL: Tyndale House Publishers, Inc., Electronic version, QuickVerse 6.0, Parsons Technology.
12. *The Believer's Study Bible*, W. A. Criswell, ed., Daniel L. Akin, New Testament ed., Criswell Center for Biblical Studies, 1991; Electronic Edition STEP Files, Cedar Rapids, IA: Parsons Technology, Inc., 1998.
13. *Ibid*.
14. Jn. 19:25b-27.
15. 1 Cor. 15:3-8.
16. Acts 1:12-14.
17. Mk. 9:1-8.
18. Acts 2:36b.
19. Acts 4:11-12.
20. 1 Pet. 2:21b-22, 24.
21. 2 Pet. 1:16-18.
22. Jn. 1:1-4, 12.
23. Jn. 1:14.

Chapter Nine

Toward Greater Union With Christ

R emember my vision I shared earlier in the book about the seven consecutive doorways? Written over the doorway of door six was "Mercy"—this dealt with God's revelation being worked into my (our) life (lives). This indeed takes a heart of great compassion to keep proceeding onward.

As the vision unfolded, I saw written over the seventh doorway the culminating words—"Union With Christ." How my heart yearned for intimacy to be wrought in my life! Since that experience, I have sought the Scriptures in a fresh way concerning this mystical marriage we often term "greater union." I asked the Lord for tutors and mentors of these ways.

Once again, the Holy Spirit has been faithful and He brought me to the epistles penned by Paul, a bond servant of the Lord Jesus Christ. Truly, this man was consumed by and with God. Next, my lovely Lord lead me by a dream in which I was taken on a journey to the St. Lawrence River, which separates Canada and the United States. I was told to dip my feet into the waters of St. Lawrence. As I was awakened from the dream, I knew an appointment awaited me through the writings of Brother Lawrence. And then there is my friend Andrew Murray. (Now I have never met him—I have just devoured his books!)

What a great Teacher we have! So let's continue reaching for the Lover of our soul by taking a drink from the waters of the Spirit as dispensed through the Lord's servants—Paul the apostolic teacher, and Brother Lawrence, a gatekeeper of His presence. Along the way, we might take a sip or two from among some of the other contemplative writers.

Paul's Mission Statement

If we were to try to identify from Paul's writings in the New Testament a "mission statement" for his life, perhaps it would be, "For to me, to live is Christ and to die is gain."[1] Paul identified himself with Christ so thoroughly that his own life was nothing by comparison. After reciting to the Philippians his "credentials" as a Jew and a Pharisee, Paul then put it in proper perspective:

But whatever things were gain to me, those things I have counted as loss for the sake of Christ. More than that, I count all things to be loss in view of the surpassing value of knowing Christ Jesus my Lord, for whom I have suffered the loss of all things, and count them but rubbish so that I may gain Christ, and may be found in Him, not having a righteousness of my own derived from the Law, but that which is through faith in Christ, the righteousness which comes from God on the basis of faith, that I may know Him and the power of His resurrection and the fellowship of His sufferings, being conformed to His death; in order that I may attain to the resurrection from the dead.[2]

All the proud self-achievements and status of his life Paul regarded as "loss" and "rubbish" next to the "surpassing value of knowing Christ." For Paul, the goal of life was union with Christ. Pursuit of that goal involved a daily process of seeking to become more and more like Christ. In Paul's eyes, union with Christ meant daily growth in Christ-likeness.

Look at the intimate way he describes this union. Paul wants not only to "gain Christ," but also to "be found *in* Him." He wants to "know" Christ, not just in head knowledge or mental awareness, but in every way. Paul wants to identify fully with Christ, both in the "power of His resurrection" and in the "fellowship of His sufferings." He is willing to take the bad along with the good because he knows that to join himself to Christ means to put himself at enmity with the world. Just as the world hated Christ, so it will hate those who follow Him. For Paul, this was just part of the "package." No one can experience full union with Christ unless he is willing to identify with Jesus' *death* as well as His *life*. That's why Paul regarded himself as being "conformed" to the death of Christ.

There is an important lesson for us in this. It is so easy to get caught up in the blessings, the gifts, and all the "feel-good" aspects of life in the Spirit that we can forget that the call to discipleship in Christ is a call to discipline, self-denial, and sacrificial living. Many Christians hunger and clamor for the former but want nothing to do with the latter. Greater union with Christ requires both. Jesus said, "If anyone wishes to come after Me, he must deny himself, and take up his cross daily and follow Me."[3] In *The Cost of Discipleship*, German pastor and theologian Dietrich Bonhoeffer writes, "When we are called to follow Christ, we are summoned to an exclusive attachment to his person."[4] He further states, "When Christ calls a man, he bids him come and die."[5]

For Paul, Christ was *All*

Some of the last words we have from the pen of Paul summarize his life: "For I am already being poured out as a drink offering, and the time of my departure has come. I have fought the good fight, I have finished the course, I have kept the faith."[6] Paul had already long since regarded his self-pursuits as "loss" and "rubbish" compared to Christ, and considered himself "dead to sin, but alive to God in Christ Jesus."[7] Now he saw himself as a "drink offering" being poured out for God. Paul considered it nothing for his life to be "wasted on Jesus," for nothing else mattered. For Paul, *to live was Christ*. Christ was his *all*.

Total Identification

This total identification with Christ permeates all of Paul's letters in the New Testament. He is always referring to it in one way or another. Consider these examples:

- *Be imitators of me, just as I also am of Christ.*[8]

- *For I determined to know nothing among you except Jesus Christ, and Him crucified.*[9]

- *I have been crucified with Christ; and it is no longer I who live, but Christ lives in me; and the life which I now live in the flesh I live by faith in the Son of God, who loved me and gave Himself up for me.*[10]

- *But may it never be that I would boast, except in the cross of our Lord Jesus Christ, through which the world has been crucified to me, and I to the world.*[11]

- *Have this attitude in yourselves which was also in Christ Jesus, who, although He existed in the form of God, did not regard equality with God a thing to be grasped, but emptied Himself, taking the form of a bond-servant, and being made in the likeness of men. Being found in appearance as a man, He humbled Himself by becoming obedient to the point of death, even death on a cross.*[12]

- *Therefore if you have been raised up with Christ, keep seeking the things above, where Christ is, seated at the right hand of God. Set your mind on the things above, not on the things that are on earth. For you have died and your life is hidden with Christ in God. When Christ, who is our life, is revealed, then you also will be revealed with Him in glory.*[13]

- *Do not lie to one another, since you laid aside the old self with its evil practices, and have put on the new self who is being renewed to a true knowledge according to the image of the One who created him— a renewal in which there is no distinction between Greek and Jew, circumcised and uncircumcised, barbarian, Scythian, slave and freeman, but Christ is all, and in all.*[14]

For Paul, the Call Was to Be Like Christ

Paul also constantly urges us in his letters to speak, think, and live in a manner that reflects the heart and mind of Christ. Let's consider some more basic Scriptures to make our foundation sure.

- *See that no one repays another with evil for evil, but always seek after that which is good for one another and for all people. Rejoice always; pray without ceasing; in everything give thanks; for this is God's will for you in Christ Jesus. Do not quench the Spirit; do not despise prophetic utterances. But examine everything carefully; hold fast to that which is good; abstain from every form of evil.*[15]

- *Let no unwholesome word proceed from your mouth, but only such a word as is good for edification according to the need of the moment, so that it will give grace to those who hear.*[16]

- *Therefore I urge you, brethren, by the mercies of God, to present your bodies a living and holy sacrifice, acceptable to God, which is your spiritual service of worship. And do not be conformed to this world, but be transformed by the renewing of your mind, so that you may prove what the will of God is, that which is good and acceptable and perfect.*[17]

- *Finally, brethren, whatever is true, whatever is honorable, whatever is right, whatever is pure, whatever is lovely, whatever is of good repute, if there is any excellence and if anything worthy of praise, dwell on these things.*[18]

Paul's emphasis on imitating Christ did not develop casually or accidentally. I believe it was, at least in part, a product of deliberate, focused attention and contemplation by Paul on the person of Jesus Christ and on His atoning work on the cross. Saul (later called Paul) ran into Jesus on the Damascus road, where our glorious intruder issued a summons for Saul to follow Him. Instinctively, Saul knew without question that receiving these enlistment papers meant giving up everything—including his own life. Such is the price for union with Christ.

Saul was driven in his pursuit of Christ-likeness. His motivation was love for his Lord and recognition of everything that Christ had done for him. In Saul's view, the only reasonable response to such divine love, grace, and mercy was a life of complete obedience and self-surrender. He considered wasting his life on Jesus a small price to pay for the Lover of his soul who had given up everything for him.

Jesus Christ Is the Beginning and the End

Paul pursued with abandonment the likeness of Christ because he realized that apart from Christ he was nothing and life was nothing. The reason that union with Christ is so important is that there is no life outside of Christ. Either He is everything or He is nothing; either He is life or He is death. By His own words Jesus Himself leaves us no reason to doubt.

- *"I am the Alpha and the Omega," says the Lord God, "who is and who was and who is to come, the Almighty."*[19]

- *I am the Alpha and the Omega, the first and the last, the beginning and the end.*[20]

- *Then He said to me, "It is done. I am the Alpha and the Omega, the beginning and the end. I will give to the one who thirsts from the spring of the water of life without cost.*[21]

- *Jesus said to them, "Truly, truly, I say to you, before Abraham was born, I am."*[22]

- *Jesus said to her, "I am the resurrection and the life; he who believes in Me will live even if he dies, and everyone who lives and believes in Me will never die. Do you believe this?"*[23]

- *Jesus said to him, "I am the way, and the truth, and the life; no one comes to the Father but through Me."[24]*

New Testament writers affirm these same truths about Jesus.

- *In Him was life, and the life was the Light of men.[25]*

- *He who has the Son has the life; he who does not have the Son of God does not have the life. These things I have written to you who believe in the name of the Son of God, so that you may know that you have eternal life.[26]*

Referring to Jesus, Peter said,

- *And there is salvation in no one else; for there is no other name under heaven that has been given among men by which we must be saved.[27]*

Why do we need union with Christ? Why should we pursue intimate communion with Him? It is only in Him that we find life. Jesus Christ is life. It is only in Him that we find purpose and meaning. Jesus Christ is Alpha and Omega. He is the beginning, the end, and everything in between. He is the prize and the goal. That's why Paul wrote,

> *Not that I have already obtained it or have already become perfect, but I press on so that I may lay hold of that for which also I was laid hold of by Christ Jesus. Brethren, I do not regard myself as having laid hold of it yet; but one thing I do: forgetting what lies behind and reaching forward to what lies ahead, I press on toward the goal for the prize of the upward call of God in Christ Jesus.[28]*

In the same vein, the writer of the Book of Hebrews exhorts us to "...lay aside every encumbrance and the sin which so easily entangles us, and let us run with endurance the race that is set before us, fixing our eyes on Jesus, the author and perfecter of faith..."[29]

Hearing the Heartbeat of God

The heartbeat is a sure sign of life. As long as the heart is beating, life is present. Jesus Christ is for us the very heartbeat of the Father. You will remember from Chapter Two how John the beloved apostle reclined on the breast of Jesus during the Last Supper. John had the privilege of hearing the heartbeat of God. Later, John would write, "No one has seen God at any time; the only begotten God who is in the bosom of the Father, He has explained *Him*."[30]

Jesus, who is "in the bosom of the Father"—He is the Father's "heartbeat"—has "explained Him." Through Jesus we know the

Father. When the Father sent Jesus to us, He sent His very best. He sent His heart. In John chapter 17, Jesus prays for everyone who believes in Him, "that they may all be one; even as You, Father, *are* in Me and I in You, that they also may be in Us…"[31] This is what greater union with Christ is all about. Because the Father and the Son are one, we become one with the Father *in* and *through* the Son. His heart now beats in us. We are in His thoughts, His mind, and His plan. God is seeking in us to fashion a mate suitable for His own heart. Holy intimacy—Holy union—Holy marriage. And what God joins together let no man separate!

Union With Christ Means Abiding in Him

Jesus Himself offers us one of the most beautiful and appropriate pictures of what union with Him means. He wants us stuck to, adhered, and fashioned to Him and Him to us!

> *Abide in Me, and I in you. As the branch cannot bear fruit of itself unless it abides in the vine, so neither can you unless you abide in Me. I am the vine, you are the branches; he who abides in Me and I in him, he bears much fruit, for apart from Me you can do nothing…If you abide in Me, and My words abide in you, ask whatever you wish, and it will be done for you. My Father is glorified by this, that you bear much fruit, and so prove to be My disciples.*[32]

The only function of a branch is to bear the fruit that is produced by the vine. Life is found in the vine, not in the branch. The vine will survive without the branch, but the branch will die without the vine. The branch shares the life of the vine as long as it is attached to and in union with the vine. Apart from Jesus we can do nothing. As long as we abide in Him, however, He produces His fruit in us. Remember the words of Paul: "But the fruit of the Spirit is love, joy, peace, patience, kindness, goodness, faithfulness, gentleness, self-control; against such things there is no law."[33] That fruit glorifies the Father and blesses the people around us. Others will know that we are in union with Christ when they see His fruit in our lives.

Give Them to Andrew

Years ago, the Lord spoke to one of my intercessory tutors—a man named Dick Simmons—a dear man of the secret place. The Lord was talking with Dick about the great harvest of souls that one day would come. The Holy Spirit said, "Give them to Andrew." Dick was not fully sure what that meant at that moment—but some years later, he realized the Lord was speaking of the purity of the words of Andrew Murray.

"Give them to Andrew." The words of this great teacher have been powerfully used to shape my own life. When I get to Heaven, one of the first people I want to meet (after Jesus, of course) is Andrew Murray. May the writings of this man and other forerunners impact you as they have me.

In his classic devotional book *Abide in Christ*, Andrew Murray describes this connection between abiding in Jesus and bearing fruit. Although written a century ago, the books of this Dutch Reformed minister from South Africa have marked my life more than those of any modern author. I praise God for the revelation he gave to Andrew Murray.

> We all know what fruit is: the produce of the branch, by which men are refreshed and nourished. The fruit is not for the good of the branch but for those who come to carry it away. As soon as the fruit is ripe, the branch gives it up, to commence afresh its work of beneficence and to anew prepare its fruit for another season. A fruit-bearing tree lives not for itself but wholly for those to whom its fruit brings refreshment and life. And so the branch exists only and entirely for the sake of the fruit. To make glad the heart of the gardener is its object, its safety, and its glory.

> Beautiful image of the believer, abiding in Christ! He not only grows in strength—the union with the Vine becoming ever surer and firmer—he also bears fruit, yea, much fruit. He has the power to offer to others that of which they can eat and live. Amid all who surround him he becomes like a tree of life, of which they can taste and be refreshed. He is in his circle a center of life and of blessing, and that simply because he abides in Christ and receives from Him the Spirit and the life, of which he can impart to others. Learn therefore, if you would bless others, to abide in Christ, and that if you do abide, you shall surely bless! As surely as the branch abiding in a fruitful vine bears fruit, so surely, yea, *much more surely*, will a soul abiding in Christ with His fullness of blessing be made a blessing![34]

One thing that Murray reminds us of here is that the Lord does not bless us solely for our own sake. He blesses us so that we can be a blessing. The inward journey of proceeding into His presence and the quietness of the soul in waiting before Him are not complete until and unless they result in the outward journey to carry the fire of His love to people who are shivering in the dark.

Union With Christ Means Learning to Practice the Presence of God

One thing that is sorely lacking in the lives of many, many Christians today is a daily, continual sense or awareness of the presence of God. Busyness of life, the allure of the world, and undisciplined lifestyles all serve to desensitize us to the Lord's presence. Learning to focus on Christ in the midst of daily life is a challenge we all face. That's what this book is all about. Remember—push the pause button.

We can take heart in the journey because we can draw on the wisdom and experience of others who have gone before us. One of these was a 17th century Frenchman named Nicholas Herman. Converted at the age of 18, Herman spent some time in the French army during the Thirty Years' War, during which he was severely wounded. Afterward, he spent many years in the service of a local official. Around the age of 50, Herman entered the Discalced Carmelite (the same order as St. Teresa of Avila) monastery in Paris as a lay brother. Renamed "Brother Lawrence," he spent the rest of his life (36 years) working among the pots and pans in the monastery kitchen. It was in the midst of these humble circumstances that Brother Lawrence learned how to practice the presence of God.

Brother Lawrence gained a wide reputation both inside and outside the monastery, and many people sought his spiritual counsel either in person or by letter. His words of wisdom and counsel are preserved in *The Practice of the Presence of God*, a classic of spiritual devotion that continues to inspire believers today.

Brother Lawrence began where we all must begin: giving ourselves wholly to God.

> Having found in many books different methods of going to God, and divers practices of the spiritual life, I thought this would serve rather to puzzle me than facilitate what I sought after, which was nothing but how to become wholly God's. This made me resolve to give the all for the all; so after having given myself wholly to God, that He might take away my sins, *I renounced, for the love of Him, everything that was not He, and I began to live as if there was none but He and I in the world.*

Sometimes I considered myself before Him as a poor crim-
inal at the feet of his judge; at other times I beheld Him in
my heart as my Father, as my God. I worshipped Him the
oftenest that I could, keeping my mind in His holy Presence, and recalling it as often as I found it wandered from
Him.[35]

As he grew in this grace of God's presence, Brother Lawrence
discovered a wonderful freedom and familiarity with God.

But when we are faithful to keep ourselves in His holy presence, and set Him always before us, this not only hinders
our offending Him and doing anything that may displease
Him, at least wilfully, but it also begets in us a holy freedom, and, if I may so speak, a familiarity with God, where-
with we ask and, that successfully, the graces we stand in
need of.

In fine, by often repeating these acts, they become *habitual*,
and the presence of God rendered as it were *natural* to us.[34]

Practicing the Presence of God
Brings Great Sweetness to the Soul

At the heart of Brother Lawrence's practice was an ongoing
"secret conversation" with God that brought him great joy and
sweetness of soul.

I have quitted all forms of devotion and set prayers but
those to which my state obliges me. And I make it my busi-
ness only to persevere in His holy presence, wherein I keep
myself by a simple attention, and a general fond regard to
God, which I may call an *actual presence* of God; or, to speak
better, an habitual, silent, and secret conversation of the
soul with God, which often causes me joys and raptures
inwardly, and sometimes also outwardly, so great that I am
forced to use means to moderate them, and prevent their
appearance to others.

My most useful method is this simple attention, and such a
general passionate regard to God, to whom I find myself
often attached with greater sweetness and delight than that
of an infant at the mother's breast; so that, if I dare use the
expression, I should choose to call this state the bosom of

God, for the inexpressible sweetness which I taste and experience there.[37]

A Warning Along the Way

However, Brother Lawrence cautions us against seeking the presence of God out of a desire for personal pleasure.

I know that for the right practice of it the heart must be empty of all other things, because God will possess the heart *alone*; and as He cannot possess it *alone* without emptying it of all besides, so neither can He act *there*, and do in it what He pleases, unless it be left vacant to Him.

There is not in the world a kind of life more sweet and delightful than that of a continual conversation with God. Those only can comprehend it who practice and experience it; yet I do not advise you to do it from that motive. It is not pleasure which we ought to seek in this exercise; but let us do it from a principle of love, and because God would have us.[38]

Practicing the Presence of God
Means That God Is Our Sole Desire

Many Christians today live humdrum lives with little awareness of or hunger for anything deeper. The same was true in Brother Lawrence's day, and he could not understand it.

I cannot imagine how religious persons can live satisfied without the practice of *the presence of God*. For my part, I keep myself retired with Him in the fund or center of my soul as much as I can; and while I am so with Him I fear nothing, but the least turning from Him is insupportable....

It is...necessary to put our whole trust in God, laying aside all other cares, and even some particular forms of devotion, though very good in themselves, yet such as one often engages in unreasonably, because those devotions are only means to attain to the end. So when by this exercise of *the presence of God* we are *with Him* who is our end, it is then useless to return to the means; but we may continue with Him our commerce of love, persevering in His holy presence, one while by an act of praise, of adoration, or of desire; one while by an act of resignation or thanksgiving; and in all the ways which our spirit can invent.[39]

Brother Lawrence said that the more we know God, the more we will love Him, and that in the final analysis, it is *faith* which will bring us closest to God.

> Let all our employment be to *know* God; the more one *knows* Him, the more one *desires* to know Him. And as *knowledge* is commonly the measure of *love*, the deeper and more extensive our *knowledge* shall be, the greater will be our love; and if our love of God were great, we should love Him equally in pains and pleasures.

> Let us not content ourselves with loving God for the mere sensible favors, how elevated soever; which He has done or may do us. Such favors, though never so great, cannot bring us so near to Him as faith does in one simple act. Let us seek Him often by faith. He is within us; seek Him not elsewhere....

> Let us begin to be devoted to Him in good earnest. Let us cast everything besides out of our hearts. He would possess them alone. Beg this favor of Him. If we do what we can on our parts, we shall soon see that change wrought in us which we aspire after.[40]

What we aspire after is union with Christ—"oneness" *with* Him and *in* Him. This is *not* the "oneness" of Buddhism's "nirvana," with its extinction of desire and individual consciousness and absorption into the universe. On the contrary, "oneness" in Christ enhances and completes our personhood. Richard Foster states it this way:

> Union with God does not mean the loss of our individuality. Far from causing any loss of identity, union brings about full personhood. We become all that God created us to be. Contemplatives sometimes speak of their union with God by the analogy of a log in a fire: the glowing log is so united with the fire that it *is* fire, while, at the same time, it remains wood. Others use the comparison of a white-hot iron in a furnace: "Our personalities are transformed, not lost, in the furnace of God's love."[41]

More Than a Gift

Union with Christ is not appropriating a gift; it is entering into intimate fellowship with a Person. For Paul, it meant becoming more like Jesus every day. For Brother Lawrence it was daily, continual communion with God. However we describe it, union with Christ is the goal of our inward journey.

Wasting your life on Jesus might be demonstrated through tears and controversial, extravagant displays of passionate worship. But the manifestation is not necessarily the fruit we gauge everything by. Is the heart on fire? Is your heart burning with desire for Him? Oh, pursue Him! Quiet your soul before Him! Let your heart pant for Him as a deer pants for the water. Ask Him to bring you into greater union with Christ Jesus.

The warmth of His great love will consume and transform us as we wait upon the Lord in His presence. Then, with the fire of His love smoldering in our hearts, we are ready for the outward journey, which will take us into the neighborhoods and the nations in lives of sacrifice and service. Oh, Father, grace us that we will only cast one shadow!

Reflection Questions

1. What does it mean to "abide in Christ"?
2. According to Brother Lawrence, how do you practice the presence of Jesus?
3. From the writings of Paul the apostle, what are some of the key Scriptures that speak of union with Christ?

Recommended Reading

Experiencing the Depths of the Lord Jesus Christ by Madame Jeanne Guyon (Whitaker House, 1994)

The Lost Passions of Jesus by Donald L. Milam, Jr. (Destiny Image, 1999)

Practicing His Presence by Brother Lawrence and Frank Laubach (Christian Books, 1973)

Endnotes

. Phil. 1:21.
2. Phil. 3:7-11.
3. Lk. 9:23b.
4. Dietrich Bonhoeffer, *The Cost of Discipleship*, New York: The Macmillan Company, 1963, p. 63.
5. *Ibid.*, p. 99.
6. 2 Tim. 4:6-7.
7. Rom. 6:11b.
8. 1 Cor. 11:1.
9. 1 Cor. 2:2.
10. Gal. 2:20.
11. Gal. 6:14.
12. Phil. 2:5-8.
13. Col. 3:1-4.
14. Col. 3:9-11.
15. 1 Thess. 5:15-22.
16. Eph. 4:29.
17. Rom. 12:1-2.
18. Phil. 4:8.
19. Rev. 1:8.
20. Rev. 22:13.
21. Rev. 21:6.
22. Jn. 8:58.
23. Jn. 11:25-26.
24. Jn. 14:6.

25. Jn. 1:4.
26. 1 Jn. 5:12-13.
27. Acts 4:12.
28. Phil. 3:12-14.
29. Heb. 12:1b-2a.
30. Jn. 1:18.
31. Jn. 17:21a.
32. Jn. 15:4-5, 7-8.
33. Gal. 5:22-23.
34. Andrew Murray, *Abide in Christ*, Springdale, PA: Whitaker House, 1979, pp. 127-128..

35. Brother Lawrence, *The Practice of the Presence of God*, in *The Treasury of Christian Spiritual Classics*, Nashville: Thomas Nelson Publishers, 1994, p. 571.
36. *Ibid.*, pp.571-72.
37. *Ibid.*, pp. 573-74.
38. *Ibid.*, pp. 576-77.
39. *Ibid.*, pp.577-78.
40. *Ibid.*, pp. 583-84.
41. Richard Foster, *Prayer: Finding the Heart's True Home*, San Francisco: Harper Collins, 1992, pp. 159-160.

Part Three

The Outward Journey: The Fire of His Love

Chapter Ten

The Fasted Life

A s we round the corner to the third and final part of this book—"The Outward Journey: The Fire of His Love"—we will build on all that we have previously studied. I will challenge you to waste your life on Jesus, by calling you into radical acts of obedience and service. But remember, any good we do is because He first touched us!

God is always at work around us. Everything He does has purpose and significance; God never does anything just to "do" something. Throughout history, whenever God has prepared to do a special work in the earth or to initiate the next step or phase of His plan, He has always revealed His intentions to those of His servants who by faith and obedience are walking in intimate fellowship with Him. When the Lord prepared to destroy Sodom and Gomorrah, He said, "Shall I hide from Abraham what I am about to do, since Abraham will surely become a great and mighty nation, and in him all the nations of the earth will be blessed?"[1] He then revealed His intentions to Abraham, resulting in Abraham's intercession for any righteous people who might be found in the twin cities.

The prophet Amos stated plainly, "Surely the Lord God does nothing / Unless He reveals His secret counsel / To His servants the prophets."[2] Even when the nation of Israel faced God's judgment time after time for their sins, He always sent His prophetic messengers to the people first to warn them of the coming judgment and to call them to repent and return to Him.

When the time approached for Jesus, God's promised Messiah, to be born, God again revealed His workings to certain of His servants who were waiting on Him quietly in faith, with their hearts tuned to His heart. He spoke to Mary and Joseph. He spoke to Elizabeth, the mother of John the Baptist, who discerned through the Holy Spirit that the child in Mary's womb was the Son of God. He spoke to Simeon and Anna, two faithful, elderly servants in Jerusalem who, upon seeing Mary and Joseph in the temple to dedicate their firstborn son to God, recognized Him as the Lord's Promised One.

Simeon was a "righteous and devout" man who had been told by the Holy Spirit that he would see "the Lord's Christ" before he died.[3] When he saw the infant Jesus, Simeon blessed God and referred to the child as "Your salvation…a light of revelation to the Gentiles, and the glory of Your people Israel."[4]

Anna Represents a Life of Radical Abandonment to God

Anna is one of my personal favorite characters mentioned in the Bible. Of Anna, the Gospel of Luke records,

> And there was a prophetess, Anna the daughter of Phanuel, of the tribe of Asher. She was advanced in years and had lived with her husband seven years after her marriage, and then as a widow to the age of eighty-four. She never left the temple, serving night and day with fastings and prayers. At that very moment she came up and began giving thanks to God, and continued to speak of Him to all those who were looking for the redemption of Jerusalem.[5]

Although this brief passage is the only mention of Anna in the entire Bible, it tells us quite a bit about her. She was a prophetess, meaning she received prophetic words and insight from the Lord. Widowed early, Anna apparently had devoted most of her life—perhaps as much as 60 years or more—to serving the Lord in the temple with "fastings and prayers." No wonder she was in touch with God! Here was a woman who gladly "wasted" herself in a lifestyle of abandoned devotion to the Lover of her soul.

When Anna saw the infant Jesus, she exuberantly thanked God and told others about the coming of the Messiah. Anna acted as though she was the one *expecting* Him! I believe she was. Anna spent her life in fasting and prayer, not just during occasional crises, but as a regular practice. Instead of morning sickness, she had a "love sickness" for God and God alone. She was one of a company of people— no one knows how many—who ministered in the temple, fasted regularly, and prayed through the prophetic promises of God, waiting expectantly for the arrival of the Messiah. I call these "prophetic intercessors." Those who *expected* Him were in a spiritual position to *recognize* Him when He came.

Anna is an example for anyone who would live an abandoned life for Christ. Just as God raised up a faithful company of servants to fast and pray before the first coming of the Messiah, so He will do again before the Second Coming of the Messiah. Once again He will call out His "Simeons" and "Annas," an end-times generation of saints who will live and walk in radical abandonment to Him. They will be a vanguard to pave the way for the restoration of God's temple—the filling up of God's collective houses of worship and the reestablishment of 24-hour houses of prayer throughout the cities of the earth.

And like Anna of old and others of her day who longed and prayed for the coming of the Messiah, the end-times "Simeons" and "Annas" will echo the cry of the saints in the closing moments of the Book of Revelation, "Come, Lord Jesus."[6]

The Church Needs to Restore the Lost Art of Fasting

Anna's daily life in the temple was not devoted only to prayer but to *fasting* and prayer. Fasting was a common practice not only among the Jews of both Old and New Testament times, but among the early Christians as well. As a spiritual discipline, fasting has been a regular part of the lives of many Christians throughout most of church history. In modern times, however, it has fallen into general disuse among believers, particularly in the West. We have become so satisfied in our culture of plenty and so addicted to our "microwave mind-set" of instant gratification that fasting seems a quaint and archaic relic of a simpler and slower past that seems gone forever.

The modern Church is poorer and leaner for neglect of the practice of fasting. Many believers suffer from spiritual anemia because they have never learned the healthy benefits of fasting as a regular discipline. When properly understood and practiced, fasting is both a powerful weapon of spiritual warfare and an indispensable aid for entering into intimacy with God. It is also a key to releasing God's presence in and through our lives. Because it helps us get in touch with God's heart and mind, fasting also assists us in preparing ourselves for the outward ministry of sharing the fire of God's love with others.

It is time for the western Church to recover the lost art of fasting. In recent years a renewed interest and emphasis on fasting has begun to appear in many parts of the Church, a renewal that transcends sectarian and denominational boundaries. One of the primary obstacles to overcome is the basic ignorance of many believers with regard to what fasting is, why it is important, and how to do it.

There is Biblical Precedent for Fasting

The earliest mention of fasting in Scripture is the 40-day fast of Moses when God met with him on Mt. Sinai.[7] During that time Moses received the Ten Commandments as well as instructions for building the tabernacle. The unique characteristic of this fast is that it was a *supernatural* fast. God divinely enabled Moses to go for 40 days without food *or* water! Later, after Moses smashed the stone tablets in anger over the Israelites' sin with the golden calf, he observed another supernatural fast in the presence of God while the tablets were replaced.[8]

The Hebrew word for fasting is *tsum*, which refers to self-denial and voluntary abstinence from food. Many scholars believe that fasting began as a loss of appetite due to times of great stress and pressure, such as when Hannah, the mother of Samuel, "wept and would not eat"[9] because of her barrenness. Fasting was a natural expression of human grief, such as when David fasted in sorrow over Abner's death.[10] Eventually, fasting evolved into a way for making one's petition effective before God. When fasting was observed on a nationwide basis in Israel, it was used to seek divine favor, protection, or to circumvent the historical judgment of God. It thus became a normal practice for a group of people to combine confession of sin, sorrow, and intercession with fasting.

The only *required* fast for all the Jewish people was the yearly fast on the Day of Atonement, when the high priest entered the Most Holy Place and offered sacrifices for the sins of the people.[11] For their part, the people fasted for self-examination and to demonstrate remorse for their sins.

By New Testament times, fasting was a familiar and well-established practice. Pharisees fasted twice a week.[12] John the Baptist and his followers fasted regularly.[13] Jesus Himself not only observed the yearly fast on the Day of Atonement as part of His Jewish heritage, but He also began His public ministry with an extended 40-day fast in the wilderness, where He was tempted by satan. Although He left little specific guidelines for His disciples concerning fasting, He did teach them that their fasting should be different from that of the Pharisees. They should fast in order to be seen by God rather than to impress men.[14] With Jesus, fasting was not a matter of "if," but "when."

Fasting was also a standard practice in the early Church, particularly before ordaining elders or setting people apart to a special task or ministry.[15] Paul and other leaders of the early Church fasted regularly.[16]

There Is Historical Precedent for Fasting

Until recent years, fasting as a spiritual discipline has been a common part of Christian practice throughout church history. According to Epiphanius, the bishop of Salamus, who was born in AD 315, Christians began early to fast twice a week, choosing Wednesdays and Fridays to avoid being confused with the Pharisees, who fasted on Tuesdays and Thursdays. Epiphanius stated, "Who does not know that the fast of the fourth and sixth days of the week are observed by Christians throughout the world?"[17]

During the 2nd and 3rd centuries, fasting was encouraged as part of the preparation for receiving water baptism. Another early development was the practice of fasting for several days before Easter as spiritual preparation for celebrating the resurrection of Jesus. This gradually evolved into Lent, the 40 days immediately prior to Easter, which was a special time of humility, self-denial, and seeking God's face.

Fasting has long been associated with spiritual reform, renewal, and revival movements. The founders and members of the medieval monastic orders practiced fasting as a regular part of their lifestyle. Each of the 16th century reformers, such as Calvin, Luther, and others, as well as leaders from earlier generations, also practiced fasting, as did the leaders of the great evangelical awakenings. John Wesley would not ordain a man to ministry unless he fasted two days every week. Jonathan Edwards, one of the principal figures in the Great Awakening in America during the 18th century, is known to have fasted before preaching his famous sermon, "Sinners in the Hands of an Angry God." When he "preached" this sermon, reading it word-for-word by the light of a single candle, people all over the congregation cried out in horror over their sins and gripped their pews tightly for fear of immediately sinking into hell! Whenever Charles Finney, the noted evangelist and revivalist of the 19th century, felt the anointing of the Holy Spirit lift from his life or preaching, he retreated and fasted until it returned.

During the Layman's Prayer Revival of North America in 1859, Christians fasted and attended prayer meetings during their lunch hours. Beginning in New York City with only a few people at one church, the movement quickly spread until in only a matter of weeks thousands of people were involved in cities all across the land, resulting in hundreds of conversions. Some historians have credited the Layman's Prayer Revival with helping to instill in America the spiritual fiber needed to survive the four bloody years of the Civil War that came soon after.

There Are Many Reasons to Fast

Many Christians who know little about fasting assume that it always means going without food for an extended period of time. While that may be the most familiar image, it is only one of many different approaches. An excellent, thorough, and inspiring treatment of the entire subject of fasting is found in Mahesh Chavda's book, *The Hidden Power of Prayer and Fasting.*[18]

Another helpful resource that has helped shape my perspective is *Fasting for Spiritual Breakthrough*, by Elmer L. Towns, in which the author identifies nine different kinds of biblical fasts.[19] The Scriptural basis is found in Isaiah:

> *Is this not the fast which I choose, / To loosen the bonds of wickedness, / To undo the bands of the yoke, / And to let the oppressed go free / And break every yoke? / Is it not to divide your bread with the hungry / And bring the homeless poor into the house; / When you see the naked, to cover him; / And not to hide yourself from your own flesh? / Then your light will break out like the dawn, / And your recovery will speedily spring forth; / And your righteousness will go before you; / The glory of the Lord will be your rear guard.*[20]

1. *The Disciple's Fast*: to "loosen the bonds of wickedness" and free ourselves and others from addictions to sin. See Matthew 17:14-21.

2. *The Ezra Fast*: to "undo the bands of the yoke," to solve problems and to invite the Holy Spirit's aid in lifting loads and overcoming barriers that keep us and our loved ones from walking joyfully with the Lord. See Ezra 8:21-23.

3. *The Samuel Fast*: to "let the oppressed go free," to win souls and bring revival, to identify with people everywhere enslaved literally or by sin, and to pray to be used of God to bring people out of the kingdom of darkness and into God's marvelous light. See First Samuel 7:1-6.

4. *The Elijah Fast*: to "break every yoke," conquer the mental and emotional problems that would control our lives, and return control to the Lord. See First Kings 19:1-8.

5. *The Widow's Fast*: to "divide [our] bread with the hungry," care for the poor, and meet the humanitarian needs of others. See First Kings 17:8-16.

6. *The Saint Paul Fast*: to allow God's "light [to] break out like the dawn," bringing clearer perspective and insight as we make crucial decisions. See Acts 9:1-19.
7. *The Daniel Fast*: so "[our] recovery will speedily spring forth," and we will gain a healthier life, or for healing. See Daniel 1:3-16.
8. *The John the Baptist Fast*: so that "[our] righteousness will go before [us]," and that our testimonies and influence for Jesus will be enhanced before others. See Luke 1:13-17.
9. *The Esther Fast*: that "the glory of the Lord will be [our] rear guard" and protect us from the evil one. See Esther 4:13-5:2.

There Are Many Ways to Fast

Fasting is not always or exclusively abstaining from food for a time. There are other ways to fast; other things that we can abstain from as a sacrifice to God. For example, here are ten contemporary issues that we might consider "fasting" before God:

1. Entertainment: movies, videos, television, radio, video games, secular dancing, etc.
2. Athletic events: professional sports and other forms of athletic recreation.
3. Reading material: magazines, books, newspapers, other news media, even Christian fiction.
4. Computers: Internet activity, e-mail, computer games, etc.
5. Speech: phone calls, limiting the amount of talking or the topics of conversation, taking a special vow of silence, abstaining from negative, critical speech.
6. Dress: avoiding certain types and styles of clothing, or the wearing of specific types and styles of clothing.
7. Foods and drinks: partial fasting, limiting one's intake of specific foods or drinks.
8. Sleep: early morning prayer, all night prayer vigils, prayer watches at various hours, etc.
9. Social functions: limiting outside engagements, conferences, seminars, and even normal church activities for short, specific periods, for times of purposeful consecration.
10. Work schedule: taking hours or days off from secular work, or even ministry engagements in order to seek God's face.[21]

Rarely, if ever, is true fasting done as an isolated exercise; in almost every case it is practiced in conjunction with one or more additional spiritual disciplines or responses. Some of the other activities that accompany biblical examples of fasting may include:

1. *Prayer.* See Ezra 8:23, Nehemiah 1:4, Psalm 35:13, Daniel 9:3, Luke 5:33.
2. *Worship.* See Nehemiah 9:1-3.
3. *Confession of sin.* See First Samuel 7:6, Nehemiah 9:1-3.
4. *Humiliation.* See Deuteronomy 9:18, Psalm 35:13; 69:10, First Kings 21:27, Nehemiah 9:1
5. *Reading the Scriptures.* See Nehemiah 9:1-3, Jeremiah 36:6, 10.
6. *Mourning.* See Second Samuel 1:12, First Kings 21:27, Esther 4:3, Nehemiah 1:4, Joel 2:12, Ezra 10:6.
7. *Weeping.* See Second Samuel 1:12, Nehemiah 1:4, Esther 4:3, Psalm 69:10, Joel 2:12.
8. *Abstinence from sexual relations.* See First Corinthians 7:5.[22]

As the End-time Church, We Need to Focus on the Bridegroom Fast

The Book of Joel presents a compelling picture of the end-time generation, a progression of *desolation, consecration,* and *restoration.*

Blow a trumpet in Zion, / And sound an alarm on My holy mountain! / Let all the inhabitants of the land tremble, / For the day of the Lord is coming; / Surely it is near, / A day of darkness and gloom, / A day of clouds and thick darkness. / As the dawn is spread over the mountains, / So there is a great and mighty people.../ A fire consumes before them / And behind them a flame burns. / The land is like the garden of Eden before them / But a desolate wilderness behind them, / And nothing at all escapes them.../ "Yet even now," declares the Lord, / Return to Me with all your heart, / And with fasting, weeping and mourning; / And rend your heart and not your garments." / Now return to the Lord your God, / For He is gracious and compassionate, / Slow to anger, abounding in lovingkindness / And relenting of evil.../ Blow a trumpet in Zion, / Consecrate a fast, proclaim a solemn assembly.../ So rejoice, O sons of Zion, / And be glad in the Lord your God; / For He has given you the early rain for your vindication. / And He has poured down for you the rain, / The early and latter rain as before.../ "It will come about after this / That I will pour out My Spirit on all mankind; / And your sons and daughters will prophesy, / Your old men will dream dreams, / Your young men will see visions. / Even on the male and female servants / I will pour out My Spirit in those days. / I will display wonders in the sky and on the earth, / Blood, fire and columns of smoke. / The sun will be turned into darkness / And the moon into blood / Before the great and awesome day of the Lord comes. / And it will come about that whoever calls on the name of the Lord / Will be delivered; / For on Mount Zion and in Jerusalem / There will be those who escape, / As the Lord has said, / Even among the survivors whom the Lord calls.[23]

First, there is desolation, the consequences of sin when the enemy ravages the people of God or the nation. Then comes the time of consecration, when the people repent and return to God. The sound of the trumpet summoned the people together to fast and pray and weep before the Lord. Finally, restoration comes as God renews His people by sending the early and the latter rain. The "latter rain" is the great outpouring of God's Spirit on His people "before the great and awesome day of the Lord comes," with a worldwide display of His glory. It is preceded by prayer and fasting by the people of God.

We can refer to this end-time fast as the "Bridegroom Fast": "And Jesus said to them, 'The attendants of the bridegroom cannot mourn as long as the bridegroom is with them, can they? But the days will come when the bridegroom is taken away from them, and then they will fast.' "[24] The focus of the Bridegroom Fast is not the outpouring of the Spirit, or even the restoration of the Church, but the glorious return of the Lord Jesus Christ—our Bridegroom.

The Bridegroom Fast Is the Fast of a Love-sick Heart

My friend Mike Bickle, the director of the International House of Prayer, has done some very insightful teaching on Matthew 9:15 and the Bridegroom Fast. He writes:

Jesus was saying that fasting is directly related to experiencing the presence of the Bridegroom. And that is, in essence, His highest purpose for this discipline: to develop in us a greater spiritual capacity for intimacy with our Bridegroom God.

Jesus assured those questioning Him that when He was taken away (through His death on the cross) they would fast because of their grief. He knew that His disciples had grown so accustomed to enjoying His presence that after He was gone they would mourn the loss of it and begin to yearn for a sense of closeness to Him. Yearning for the one you love is commonly called love sickness. Can you imagine whole-hearted lovers of Jesus today becoming so filled with holy lovesickness that they freely choose to live fasted lifestyles? This is what Jesus was prophetically speaking of.[25]

Mike goes on to offer three practical results that we can expect from the Bridegroom Fast:

1. You will receive more revelation of God while poring over His Word. Imagine receiving more revelation of the beauty of God that fascinates our hearts!

2. You will receive a greater measure of revelation in an accelerated way. When people tell me, "I just can't wait to receive more from God," I tell them to add fasting to their loving meditation on the Word. This type of fasting speeds up the process of receiving from God. It also speeds up the process of getting rid of old mindsets, old strongholds, and half-heartedness.

3. The revelation we receive will touch us at a deeper level. A heart tenderized in love is the greatest gift the Holy Spirit can work in a worshiper. To live feeling loved by God and feeling a reciprocal, passionate love for Him is the most exhilarating form of existence. If you want to experience more of Jesus in a deeper way, start fasting with a focus on Jesus as the Bridegroom God. The Holy Spirit gives grace and revelation to His people who aren't afraid to cry out for it. And when you respond to His wooing and embrace a Bridegroom fast—God's feast for His bride—you will mature and enter into intimacy with the Bridegroom. Then you will be able to assume your true identity as the bride of Christ and be fully prepared for His return.[26]

The Time for the Bridegroom Fast Is *Now*

We who are in Christ have a new heart and a new motivation for fasting: a hunger and longing for the return of our Bridegroom. The late Arthur Wallis penned one of the greatest classic books on fasting called *God's Chosen Fast*. His words capture for us the spirit and the urgency of the Bridegroom Fast.

Before the Bridegroom left them, He promised that He would come again to receive them to Himself. The Church still awaits the midnight cry, *"Behold the Bridegroom! Come out to meet Him!"* (Mt. 25:6) It is this age of the Church that is the period of the absent Bridegroom. It is this age of the church to which our Master referred when He said, *"then they will fast."* The time is now!

These words of Jesus were prophetic. The first Christians fulfilled them, and so have many saintly men and women of succeeding generations. Where are those who fulfill them today? Alas, they are few and far between, an exception rather than the rule, to the great loss of the Church.

A new generation, however, is arising. There is concern in the hearts of many for the recovery of apostolic power. But how can we recover apostolic power while neglecting apostolic practice? How can we expect the power to flow if we do not prepare the channels? Fasting is a God appointed means for the flowing of His grace and power that we can't afford to neglect any longer.

The fast of this age is not merely an act of mourning for Christ's absence, but an act of preparation for His return. May those prophetic words, "Then they will fast," be finally fulfilled in this generation. It will be a fasting and praying Church that will hear the thrilling cry, *"Behold, the Bridegroom!"* Tears shall then be wiped away, and the fast will be followed by the feast of the marriage supper of the Lamb.

The Spirit and the Bride say, "Come"... "Surely, I am coming soon." Amen. Come, Lord Jesus! (Rev. 22:17a, 20)[27]

We Fast Because We Love Him!

Contemplative Christians fast from a different motivation: a lovesick heart passionate for His presence and longing for His return. I believe that the bridegroom fast is a revelation for us. I believe that we will still fast for all of the other reasons—power, crisis intervention, deliverance, etc.—but we will fast first and foremost because our heart is lovesick for our Messiah. Wasting our life on our Beloved isn't even a question of great sacrifice for these lovers! They gladly waste everything on Jesus.

We will fast because we love Him and want to be near Him. We will fast because, more than anything else in this life, *we want Him!* Amen. Come, Lord Jesus! Even so, come, Lord Jesus Christ.

Reflection Questions

1. Give a biblical example of fasting for crisis intervention.
2. In addition to food, what are some things one could abstain from for spiritual purposes?
3. What is the Bridegroom Fast and how does it differ from the other models?

Recommended Reading

The Hidden Power of Prayer and Fasting by Mahesh Chavda (Destiny Image, 1998)

Fasting for Spiritual Breakthrough by Elmer Towns (Regal Books, 1966)

God's Chosen Fast by Arthur Wallis (Christian Literature Crusdae, 1968)

Endnotes

1. Gen. 18:17b-18.
2. Amos 3:7.
3. Lk. 2:25-26.
4. Lk. 2:30b 32.
5. Lk. 2:36-38.
6. Rev. 22:20b.
7. See Ex. 34:28; Deut. 9:9.
8. See Ex. 34:1-28; Deut. 9:18.
9. 1 Sam. 1:7b.
10. See 2 Sam. 3:26-37.
11. See Lev. 16.
12. See Lk. 18:11-12.
13. See Mt. 9:14-15.
14. See Mt. 6:16-18.
15. See Acts 13:2.
16. See 1 Cor. 7:5; 2 Cor. 6:5.
17. Epiphanius, Elmer L. Towns, *Fasting for Spiritual Breakthrough*, Ventura, CA: Regal Books, 1996, pp. 26.
18. Mahesh Chavda, *The Hidden Power of Prayer and Fasting*, Shippensburg, PA: Destiny Image Publishers, Inc., 1998.
19. Elmer L. Towns, *Fasting for Spiritual Breakthrough*, Ventura, CA: Regal Books, 1996, pp. 20-23.
20. Is. 58:6-8.
21. Towns, *Fasting for Spiritual Breakthrough*, pp. 228-231.
22. *Ibid.*
23. Joel 2:1-2a, 3, 12-13, 15, 23, 28-32.
24. Mt. 9:15.
25. Mike Bickle, "The Bridegroom's Fast," *Charisma*, March 2000, p. 16.
26. *Ibid.*
27. Arthur Wallis, *God's Chosen Fast*, Fort Washington, PA: Christian Literature Crusade, 1977, pp. 25-26.

Chapter Eleven

Walking Through the Tabernacle

Have you ever had a "close encounter" with the divine? Moses did, at the burning bush, when the purpose for his entire life was set in motion.[1] Jacob did, on the banks of the Jabbok River, when he lost a wrestling match but won a new name.[2] Isaiah did, the day he took up the prophet's mantle and became a spokesman for the Lord.[3]

Such a personal divine encounter was probably far from the mind of the old priest Zacharias when he entered the Holy Place in Herod's temple to offer up incense to the Lord.

> In the days of Herod, king of Judea, there was a priest named Zacharias, of the division of Abijah; and he had a wife from the daughters of Aaron, and her name was Elizabeth. They were both righteous in the sight of God, walking blamelessly in all the commandments and requirements of the Lord. But they had no child, because Elizabeth was barren, and they were both advanced in years.
>
> Now it happened that while he was performing his priestly service before God in the appointed order of his division, according to the custom of the priestly office, he was chosen by lot to enter the temple of the Lord and burn incense. And the whole multitude of the people were in prayer outside at the hour of the incense offering.[4]

In Zacharias's generation, words from the Lord were rare. There had been no prophet in the land since Malachi, over four centuries earlier. Not only that, in Jewish society of the day childlessness was considered a curse from God. Undoubtedly, two people as righteous and devoted as Zacharias and his wife, Elizabeth, had prayed for a child over and over for years, to no avail. So Zacharias had no reason to expect a personal visitation. Besides, he was probably too caught up in the uniqueness of the moment and in his concern to perform everything in exact adherence to God's law.

Zacharias's chance to offer incense in the temple was a once-in-a-lifetime opportunity. The priests were organized into 24 divisions that rotated their service at the temple, each division serving for one week twice a year. There were as many as 18,000 priests or more who served during the year. Priests were chosen by lot to enter the Holy Place to offer incense, so the privilege came *only once* in the life of any priest. The biggest moment in Zacharias's life as a priest had come, and he wanted to make sure he did everything right.

When Zacharias Approached God, God Approached Zacharias

Every aspect of the daily sacrifices and worship in the temple was governed by detailed and specific instructions that had been in place since the days of Moses. Carelessness or violations could result in death to the priest and disaster to the people. A conscientious priest took every possible precaution to avoid offending the Holy Presence.

Certainly Zacharias must have had all of these things in mind as he approached the altar of incense. As the smoke from the incense ascended, symbolic of the prayers for the forgiveness and atonement of the people, perhaps Zacharias whispered another prayer for himself and Elizabeth, that the Lord might give them a child. He wasn't prepared for what happened next.

> *And an angel of the Lord appeared to him, standing to the right of the altar of incense. Zacharias was troubled when he saw the angel, and fear gripped him. But the angel said to him, "Do not be afraid, Zacharias, for your petition has been heard, and your wife Elizabeth will bear you a son, and you will give him the name John. You will have joy and gladness, and many will rejoice at his birth. For he will be great in the sight of the Lord; and he will drink no wine or liquor, and he will be filled with the Holy Spirit while yet in his mother's womb. And he will turn many of the sons of Israel back to the Lord their God. It is he who will go as a forerunner before Him in the spirit and power of Elijah, to turn the hearts of the fathers back to the children, and the disobedient to the attitude of the righteous, so as to make ready a people prepared for the Lord."*[5]

As Zacharias performed his once-in-a-lifetime priestly service, he received a once-in-a-lifetime visitation. God's timing is always perfect. When better to answer the old priest's greatest personal heart cry than during the highest point of his priestly life? When Zacharias approached God, God approached Zacharias.

Zacharias' approach to the Lord was a carefully orchestrated process.

> The incensing priest and his assistants went first to the altar of burnt-offering, and filled a golden censer with incense, and placed burning coals from the altar in a golden bowl. As they passed into the court from the Holy Place they struck a large instrument called the *Magrephah*, which summoned all the ministers to their places. Ascending the steps to the holy place, the priests spread the coals on the golden altar, and arranged the incense, and the chief officiating priest was then left alone within the Holy Place to await the signal of the president to burn the incense. It was probably at this time that the angel appeared to Zacharias. When the signal was given, the whole multitude withdrew from the inner court, and fell down before the Lord. Silence pervaded the temple, while within, the clouds of incense rose up before Jehovah.[6]

God sent Gabriel to give personal and direct word to Zacharias that his prayer had been answered. He and Elizabeth would have a son who would grow up to be the first prophet in over four hundred years, and the forerunner of the Messiah. John the Baptist would prepare the way for Jesus.

It was not careful ritual observance alone that allowed Zacharias to approach the Lord successfully. His preparation was the work of a lifetime. The Scriptures describe both Zacharias and Elizabeth as "righteous in the sight of God, walking blamelessly in all the commandments and requirements of the Lord." Their ability to come near to God began with a lifestyle of submission and obedience to Him out of love.

The Design of the Tabernacle Gives Us a Pattern for Approaching God

Throughout this book we have been talking about approaching God—coming near to Him in intimate relationship through contemplative prayer. Because of the nature of the subject, much of the discussion has been somewhat abstract. Concrete models that we can visualize are always helpful. The design of the original tabernacle that God gave to Moses illustrates for us the divine pattern for approaching God.

Moses' tabernacle consisted of three sections, or compartments: the outer court, the inner court or Holy Place, and the Most Holy Place. Each section contained certain pieces of furniture designated for specific purposes. The outer court held the brazen altar for sacrifices and a laver of water for cleansing. Inside the Holy Place were the seven-branched candlestick, the table of shewbread, and the altar of incense. Beyond the inner veil, in the Most Holy Place, is where the Ark of the Covenant rested, with its gold mercy seat overarched by two golden cherubim. The Ark of the Covenant represented the very presence of God among His people. It contained the stone tablets of the Ten Commandments, some manna from the wilderness, and Aaron's rod that budded. The tablets represented the *Word* of God, the manna the *provision* of God, and Aaron's rod the *authority* of God.

No one except the high priest could enter the Most Holy Place, and he only once a year, on the Day of Atonement. The instructions given in the Law for the high priest to observe on the Day of Atonement reveal a specific progression into the presence of God.

As I wrote in my book *The Lost Art of Intercession*,

> ...before the high priest could pass through the inner veil into the Most Holy Place or Holy of Holies, he was to minister at two stations in the outer court and three within the Holy Place. First, he would offer up the sacrifice of blood at the brazen altar. This was followed by the ceremonial washing of water at the laver. After entering the Holy Place through the outer veil, the priest would approach the lamp stand (holding seven golden candlesticks). The table of shewbread preceded a golden altar of incense which rested immediately in front of the inner veil. Beyond the veil in the Most Holy Place was the ark of the covenant, with the mercy seat flanked by its covering cherubs. This was the place of communion—the place where God's Presence was manifested and His glory was made known.[7]

The Tabernacle Was Just a Type—*We* Are Now the Temple of God

The Tabernacle and its furnishings, along with the ritual sacrifices and cleansing of the Day of Atonement, were all types and prefigures of the atoning work that would be accomplished for all time by Jesus Christ when He died on the cross. We know from the Book of Hebrews that Christ is our great high priest who has forever fulfilled everything that the Tabernacle anticipated.

Therefore, since we have a great high priest who has gone through the heavens, Jesus the Son of God, let us hold firmly to the faith we profess. For we do not have a high priest who is unable to sympathize with our weaknesses, but we have one who has been tempted in every way, just as we are—yet was without sin. Let us then approach the throne of grace with confidence, so that we may receive mercy and find grace to help us in our time of need.[8]

With His death, Jesus opened the way to the Father. The veil is torn, and we now have direct access to the Most Holy Place. In the five-stage progression of the high priest through the tabernacle we see:

1. The brazen altar of sacrifice—being washed in the blood of the Lamb (Jesus).
2. The laver of water—being washed in the water of God's Word.
3. The seven lamps of the candlestick—being "lit" by the "seven Spirits" of God.[9]
4. The table of shewbread—fellowship of the body of Christ with the bread of His presence.
5. The altar of incense—the ministry of prayer.

It is the ministry of prayer which is closest to the heart of God. That is why the altar of incense stood directly in front of the veil leading into the Most Holy Place. It was a symbol of how we move from prayer to His presence.

The apostle Paul makes it clear that as believers, we are now the temple of God.

Don't you know that you yourselves are God's temple and that God's Spirit lives in you? If anyone destroys God's temple, God will destroy him; for God's temple is sacred, and you are that temple.[10]

Do you not know that your body is a temple of the Holy Spirit, who is in you, whom you have received from God? You are not your own; you were bought at a price. Therefore honor God with your body.[11]

We are the temple of the living God, the ark of His dwelling. As believers, we are carriers of His presence and priests in the service of our King. Simon Peter wrote that we are "a chosen race, a royal priesthood, a holy nation, a people for God's own possession."[12]

As Priests, We Are Watchmen for the Lord

As priests, we offer up to God a ministry of prayer, of which there are several models. One of these is contemplative prayer, which is the primary subject of this book. Contemplative prayer is *passive*, or *reflective* prayer, the kind where we pull the windowshades down, close the curtains, shut the doors, and retreat into our inward place with no one but God and ourselves. It's a lot like the teaching of Jesus where He tells us to go into our inner chamber, shut the door, and pray to our Father in secret. Contemplative prayer is what we call the inward journey of proceeding into His presence.

Another model of prayer is that of reminding God of His Word. We could call this model a *responsive* form of prayer, because we respond to God's promises in His Word and ask Him to move and act in response to and in keeping with His Word. A third model, which is a combination of the first two, is what I call *prophetic intercession*. It could be classified as an *aggressive* form of prayer.

What do I mean when I talk of reminding God of His Word? Another way of looking at it is to think of ourselves as watchmen for the Lord, as stated in Isaiah:

> On your walls, O Jerusalem, I have appointed watchmen; / All day and all night they will never keep silent. / You who remind the Lord, take no rest for yourselves; / And give Him no rest until He establishes / And makes Jerusalem a praise in the earth.[13]

There's a very interesting phrase in that passage: "You who *remind the Lord*." Remind Him of what? Does God forget things? Does He suffer from spiritual amnesia? Of course not. The rest of the verse says that we are not to rest, nor give *God* any rest until "He establishes and makes Jerusalem a praise in the earth." This is a reference to specific promises God made concerning Jerusalem and Israel, which I believe relate literally to Israel and spiritually to the Church. Reminding God means that we, as watchmen on the walls, bring before Him in prayer His own words and, in humility and faith, ask Him to fulfill and honor His promises. Reminding God is not an act of defiance or challenge, but of faith; it shows that we believe God, and trust Him to do everything He has promised to do.

A good biblical example of this kind of prayer is found in Psalm 74:1-2:

> O God, why have You rejected us forever? / Why does Your anger smoke against the sheep of Your pasture? / Remember Your

congregation, which You have purchased of old, / Which You have redeemed to be the tribe of Your inheritance; / And this Mount Zion, where You have dwelt.

Have you ever felt rejected by God? Does it ever seem as though you are in the middle of a spiritual desert with no oasis in sight? That's how the psalmist felt. In the midst of his depression he reminds God of two things: "Remember Your congregation…And…Mount Zion…" In this way he is asking God to move for the sake of His people, the remnant who have remained faithful to Him.

There Are at Least Seven Ways We Can Remind God

What are we to remind God of? In his classic book *Mighty Prevailing Prayer*, Wesley L. Duewel presents seven things:[14]

1. Plead the honor and glory of God's name. Throughout the Bible, this is one of the main appeals that intercessory priestly people made before God. They reminded God of His name and glory and appealed for Him to act on behalf of the honor of His name.
2. Plead God's relationship to us. We are God's children, and we have the right to appeal to Him on that basis.
3. Plead God's attributes. We can appeal to God based on His lovingkindness, His mercy, His faithfulness, His goodness, etc.
4. Plead the sorrows and needs of the people.
5. Plead the past answers to prayer. Sometimes it helps to rehearse history; to recall God's faithfulness in the past as the basis for appealing to His action in the present. This is a great faith builder.
6. Plead the Word and the promises of God.
7. Plead the blood of Jesus. The great preacher Charles Haddon Spurgeon called this one the key that will unlock any door. We remind God by speaking of the qualities of the blood of Jesus to bring forgiveness, healing, cleansing, redemption, sanctification, and direct access to God's throne of grace.

Before We Can Remind God of His Word, We Must Know His Word

It's kind of hard to remind God of what He said if we don't *know* what He said. The only way we can *know* what God said is to read, study, and meditate on His Word. If we are ever to be effective watchmen on the walls, we must become *intimately* acquainted with God's precious book of promises, the Bible.

Andrew Murray relates the close and important connection between prayer and God's Word in his great classic *With Christ in the School of Prayer.*

> *If ye abide in Me, and My words abide in you, ye shall ask what ye will, and it shall be done unto you.* (John 15:7 KJV)

> The vital connection between the Word and prayer is one of the simplest and earliest lessons of the Christian life. As the newly-converted heathen put it, "I pray—I speak to my Father; I read—my Father speaks to me." Before prayer, God's Word strengthens me by giving my faith its justification and petition. In prayer, God's Word prepares me by revealing what the Father wants me to ask. After prayer, God's Word brings me the answer, for in it the Spirit allows me to hear the Father's voice.

> It is the connection between His Word and our prayers that Jesus points to when He says, *If ye abide in Me, and My Words abide in you, ye shall ask whatever ye will, and it shall be done unto you.* The deep importance of this truth becomes clear if we notice the expression which this one replaces. More than once Jesus said, *Abide in Me and I in you.* His abiding in us was the complement and the crown of our abiding in Him. But here, instead of Ye in Me and I in you, He says, Ye in Me and My words in you. The abiding of His Words is the equivalent of Himself abiding.

> God is the infinite Being in whom everything is life, power, spirit and truth—in the very deepest meaning of the words. When God reveals Himself in His Words, He does indeed give Himself—His love and His life, His will and His power—to those who receive these words, in a reality that surpasses our comprehension. In every promise, He gives us the power to grasp and possess Himself. In every command, He allows us to share His will, His holiness, and His perfection. God's Word gives us God Himself!

> That Word is nothing less than the Eternal Son, Christ Jesus. Therefore, all of Christ's words are God's words, full of a Divine and quickening life and power. *The words I speak unto you, they are spirit and they are life. If My words abide in*

you. The condition is simple and clear. In His words, His will is revealed. As the words abide in me, His will rules me. My will becomes the empty vessel which His will fills, and the willing instrument which His will rules.[15]

Contemplative Prayer + Scriptural Praying = Prophetic Intercession

When it comes to prayer, there are many distinct specialty graces or anointings that the Spirit gives to different people. For instance, there is the general prayer person, who does great praying through prayer lists. Then there are those with a special anointing to pray for Israel. We are all supposed to pray for the peace of Jerusalem, but these Israel "prayeroholics" have a specific and focused burden for Israel and the Jewish people.

Others have the anointing to pray for those in authority. These are the folks who could tell you the names of all the national leaders of the world, as well as the names and locations of their countries. Believers with the missionary prayer anointing have a special burden and gift for interceding for Christian missionaries around the world. Revival prayer people focus on the issue of seeing the glory of God returned to the house of God. Crisis intercessors are the ones who know or sense when something is brewing, or when something cataclysmic or monumental is about to break out, and they take it before the Lord in focused intercession.

When we wed or unite quiet, communal prayer with reminding God of His Word, revelatory prayer, or *prophetic intercession*, is born. Prophetic intercession is where we shed *our* thoughts and opinions and agree and ask in *Jesus'* name. In this way, we touch Jesus and He touches us. "Again I say to you, that if two of you agree on earth about anything that they may ask, it shall be done for them by My Father who is in heaven. For where two or three have gathered together in My name, I am there in their midst."[16]

In prophetic intercession we pick up the revelatory heart of God about a matter and in utter dependency pray it back to the Father, birthing the promise into being. In this we are nothing more than clay vessels through which He flows as we kneel on the promises.

It's difficult to explain, but it's almost like going through a tunnel, or a gate. As we approach God through contemplative prayer, we draw progressively nearer to Him like the high priest making his way along the five stations in the tabernacle as he approaches the Most Holy Place.

Eventually, we enter that bright, clean, holy place where God dwells, and we sit quietly in awe and silence and pure worship. Like John the beloved, we put our ear to His chest and hear the beating of His heart. Soon we notice that our own heart has begun to beat in synchronous rhythm to His—the heartbeat of God is now beating in our heart. It might be simply for communion; God may be looking for a friend to sit with Him and chat. On the other hand, there may be a crisis brewing, and the rhythm we feel may be a burden for the breaking of revival, or for the salvation of the lost.

Whatever it is, our heart is now beating as one with God's heart, and out of that place of quiet communion the revelatory release of God's heart enters into our spirit. It might be in the form of a prophecy, or a vision, or a trance. Maybe it comes in the form of speaking back to the Father that which He has placed in us—reminding God. It might show up in the form of a spirit language through the gift of tongues as the only way to voice an agony, a love, an ecstasy, a desire, or an urgency that is too great or too deep to be expressed in human words. Perhaps it is more of a "Romans 8" experience, where we come to realize our total dependency upon God, because we do not know how to pray as we should unless the Holy Spirit reveals it to us. We reach deep inside and are reminded that the Holy Spirit has taken up residence in us, and has come alongside to help. He now intercedes for us and through us in ways that go beyond the comprehension of our mind.

Prophetic intercession asks not merely that men might make decisions for Christ. It assumes the larger boundary of the great purposes of God. We plead for the maturity of Christ to be formed in those who respond, and that the new society of redeemed mankind expands to the ends of the earth. Whether it is preached truth, prayed burden, or spontaneous utterance, it is prophetic only if it brings our generation into knowledge of the heart of God for our time.

Prophetic Intercession Paves the Way for Fulfillment of Prophetic Promises

God is looking for us to bring our hearts, our minds, and our lives into full agreement with His Word. Prophetic intercession helps us do that. It is the ability to receive an immediate prayer request from God and pray about it in a divinely anointed utterance. Prophetic intercession is waiting before God in order to "hear" or receive God's burden—His Word, warning, vision, or promises—

responding back to the Lord and then to the people with appropriate actions.

Prophetic intercession paves the way for the fulfillment of God's prophetic promises. The Spirit of God pleads the covenant promises of God made to His people throughout history. In prophetic intercession, we plead before the throne for every yet-unfulfilled promise of God.

Often, the Spirit of God will prompt us to pray for situations or circumstances about which we may possess little knowledge in the natural. Thus, we are praying for the things that are on God's heart. He "nudges" us to pray so He can intervene. When we pray according to the Spirit's prompting, the will of God will be brought forth on earth as it is in Heaven. This is a form of "birthing" in prayer. Out of a sweet intimacy a conception of God's love takes place. Then this burden—or child within—grows until it comes to the hour of labor and travail. (For more on the subject of prophetic intercession, see my book *Kneeling on the Promises—Birthing God's Purposes Through Prophetic Intercession*.)

The Way In Is Now the Way Back Out

Once the high priest made his progressive approach to the presence of God, he did not remain forever in the Most Holy Place, although I'm sure he would have liked to. He had to turn around and pass back through the veil, past the altar of incense, past the table of shewbread, past the golden lampstand, past the laver, and past the brazen altar of sacrifice, back into the world where people lived.

The same is true in our lives. We must learn this path of walking through the tabernacle into the amazing place of His glorious presence. Then we must carry that presence back out to a waiting world. One thing is certain: we will not go out the same person we were when we went in! We will have been changed, completely transformed by His radiant glory, and we will carry the essence of that glory wherever we go.

Once we have learned to take this "road less traveled," we will find it easier each time to pass through the din of many voices and to quiet our souls before the Lord and commune with Him. Why? After once we have tasted the goodness of the Lord, we won't be able to wait to go back in!

Yes, the *inward* is for the *outward*. Mary and Martha can kiss one another. We can learn the consecrated path of contemplative prayer by looking at the Old Testament shadow of walking through the tabernacle and, like the priests of old, pick up the fragrance of the smoke on our garments and carry it (Him) to a world that is aching to see, touch, and know the love of God.

Reflection Questions

1. List the consecutive stations where the Old Testament priest ministered.
2. According to the New Covenant, what do these Old Testament stations shadow or symbolize for us?
3. We are now the temple of God. Relate the teachings of the Tabernacle to our being God's dwelling place today.

Recommended Reading

The Tabernacle of Moses by Kevin Conner (Bible Temple Publications, 1980)
Secrets of the Most Holy Place by Don Nori (Destiny Image, 1992)
Beyond the Veil by Alice Smith (Regal Books)

Endnotes

1. See Ex. 3:1-10.
2. See Gen. 32:22-28.
3. See Is. 6:1-8.
4. Lk. 1:5-10.
5. Lk. 1:11-17.
6. Marvin R. Vincent, *Vincent's Word Studies, vol. 1, Synoptic Gospels*, Hiawatha, IA: Parsons Technology, Inc., Electronic Edition STEP Files, 1998.
7. Jim W. Goll, *The Lost Art of Intercession*, Shippensburg, PA: Revival Press, An Imprint of Destiny Image Publishers, Inc., 1997, p. 15.
8. Heb. 4:14-16 NIV.
9. See Rev. 1:4; 3:1; 4:5; 5:6.
10. 1 Cor. 3:16-17 NIV.
11. 1 Cor. 6:19-20 NIV.
12. 1 Pet. 2:9a.
13. Is. 62:6-7.
14. As inspired by Wesley L. Duewel, *Mighty Prevailing Prayer*, Grand Rapids, MI: Zondervan Publishing House, 1990, pp. 301-308.
15. Andrew Murray, *With Christ in the School of Prayer*, Springdale: Whitaker House, 1981, pp. 161-162.
16. Mt. 18:19-20.

Chapter Twelve

Live Coals of Fire

No one who makes the inward journey to the place of intimate communion with the Lord will ever be the same when he comes out. That innermost chamber of our hearts where we meet Him one-on-one is a place not only of sweet fellowship, but of glorious transformation also. Like St. Teresa's silkworm, we enter that realm as humble, earthbound souls only to emerge as beautiful butterflies, with our spirits ready to take wing and soar.

One of the basic lessons of science is the difference between physical and chemical changes in matter. In a physical change, the physical *state* of matter changes—ice to water to steam for example—but the chemical composition does not change. Water is still H_2O no matter what state it is in. In a chemical change, on the other hand, not only the *state* but also the *chemical makeup* of the matter is changed. As a piece of wood that is added to a fire begins to burn, it becomes one with the fire, being transformed into light and heat energy. In the process, it is consumed and changed into something it was not before: carbon ash. It will never be a piece of wood again. In a chemical change, the *essential nature* of the object is transformed; it can *never* go back to what it was before.

In Chapter Nine I quoted Richard Foster, who said, "Contemplatives sometimes speak of their union with God by the analogy of a log in a fire; the glowing log is so united with the fire that it is fire, while, at the same time, it remains wood." There, he was talking about our individual personhood. When we encounter the Lord, our individuality is not lost, but our *human nature* is totally transformed.

We can never go back to the way we were before. Our hearts are ignited by the fire of God, and we are never again the same.

Here Am I, Send Me!

The prophet Isaiah discovered for himself the transforming nature of the Lord's fire. Here is his description of the divine "close encounter" that changed him forever:

> In the year of King Uzziah's death I saw the Lord sitting on a throne, lofty and exalted, with the train of His robe filling the temple. Seraphim stood above Him, each having six wings: with two he covered his face, and with two he covered his feet, and with two he flew. And one called out to another and said,
>
> "Holy, Holy, Holy, is the Lord of hosts, / The whole earth is full of His glory."
>
> And the foundations of the thresholds trembled at the voice of him who called out, while the temple was filling with smoke. Then I said,
>
> "Woe is me, for I am ruined! / Because I am a man of unclean lips, / And I live among a people of unclean lips; / For my eyes have seen the King, the Lord of hosts."
>
> Then one of the seraphim flew to me with a burning coal in his hand, which he had taken from the altar with tongs. He touched my mouth with it and said, "Behold, this has touched your lips; and your iniquity is taken away and your sin is forgiven."
>
> Then I heard the voice of the Lord, saying, "Whom shall I send, and who will go for Us?" Then I said, "Here am I. Send me!"[1]

Isaiah's vision of the Lord in all His glory threw him into dread and despair because in that moment he recognized his own sinfulness and wickedness. He expected at any second to be struck dead by the holiness of the Almighty. Instead, Isaiah learned the love, grace, and mercy of God in a new and deeper way than ever before.

What changed Isaiah's life was the touch of the "burning coal" from the Lord's altar. Notice that the fire of the Lord touched Isaiah *at the exact point of his confession.* After he said, "I am a man of unclean lips," the burning coal was applied to his lips. In that instant, Isaiah's iniquity was taken away and his sin forgiven. His "unclean lips" were transformed into God-anointed lips for speaking the Word of the Lord.

The lips are among the most sensitive parts of the human body. Try to imagine for a moment the pain of having your lips seared with a red-hot coal! So often, the Lord's touch in our lives is painful, but in the pain there is healing. Isaiah needed the touch of the burning coal of God's fire to cauterize the wounds of his sin and his broken spirit.

That's why confession is such an important part of our walk with the Lord, particularly if we wish to pursue the inward journey. We need God to take the burning coal of His love and touch us at every point of our brokenness, and in so doing, transform us into flame-tempered vessels prepared to carry His fire.

Isaiah left the temple that day a changed man. Like a log consigned to the flames, he was to his dying day consumed by the fire of the Lord, calling God's people to repent and return to Him.

"Were Not Our Hearts Burning Within Us...?"

One of my favorite chapters in the Bible is the 24th chapter of Luke. In many ways, this chapter has guided much of my walk with the Lord over the last 25 years. What has particularly captured my attention all those years is the account Luke relates of two disciples who meet Jesus on the road to Emmaus. It is late on the day of His resurrection.

And behold, two of them were going that very day to a village named Emmaus, which was about seven miles from Jerusalem. And they were talking with each other about all these things which had taken place. While they were talking and discussing, Jesus Himself approached and began traveling with them. But their eyes were prevented from recognizing Him.[2]

As these two disciples make their way from Jerusalem to Emmaus, they discuss the unbelievable events of that weekend: the crucifixion, death, and burial of their Master, Jesus, and the reports from some of His resurrection. Before long, the risen Jesus Himself joins them on the road, but for some reason they do not recognize Him. When Jesus asks them what they have been talking about, they relate to Him everything that has happened and all that they have heard. Apparently, there is doubt in their hearts about it all, because Jesus rebukes them for their slowness to believe.

Then beginning with Moses and with all the prophets, He explained to them the things concerning Himself in all the Scriptures.

And they approached the village where they were going, and He acted as though He were going farther. But they urged Him, saying, "Stay with us, for it is getting toward evening, and the day is now nearly over." So He went in to stay with them. When He had reclined at the table with them, He took the bread and blessed it, and breaking it, He began giving it to them. Then their eyes were opened and they recognized Him; and He vanished from their sight. They said to one another, "Were not our hearts burning within us while He was speaking to us on the road, while He was explaining the Scriptures to us?"[3]

Without identifying Himself, Jesus explained to the two disciples all that the Scriptures said concerning Him. By the time the three of them reached Emmaus, it was getting late. Jesus "acted as though He were going farther," but in the hospitality of the day the two disciples invited Him to stay with them for the night. Isn't that just the way the Lord works? Sometimes it seems as though He is standing still, waiting for us to join Him. At other times, He acts as though He is going on, just to see if we will capture Him and take hold of Him. As my dear friend Tommy Tenney emphasizes—be a God chaser!

During dinner, Jesus blessed the bread and broke it, and it was in that familiar act of communion and fellowship that their eyes were opened and they recognized Him. As soon as they knew who He was, He vanished from their sight. Notice what the two disciples said to each other. *"Were not our hearts burning within us* while He was speaking to us on the road, while He was explaining the Scriptures to us?" Their hearts burned within as Jesus unfolded to them prophetic revelation concerning Himself from the Word of God.

When Jesus vanished, where did He go? I think I have an idea. The reason their hearts were burning was because Someone was taking up residence within them. Their hearts burned within because the Spirit of revelation opened their eyes to understand the Scriptures. With their spiritual eyes open, they then knew Him in the breaking of the bread. What this is saying is that they met Him in communion. When He vanished from their sight, they were left with the fire of God—*living coals of fire*—in their hearts.

It's Time for "Christian Faith 101"

Breaking of the bread is one of the most intimate acts of fellowship that we have either with one another or with our Lord. When the risen Jesus broke bread with the two disciples in Emmaus, it was a symbolic act as much as a literal one. All afternoon He had "broken the bread" of Scripture for them, feeding their hungry souls and giving them understanding. In the final, literal act of breaking bread, their understanding was complete, and they recognized Jesus for who He was—the Bread of Life.

Jesus had opened a repository in their hearts and filled it with His Word. Their hearts, minds, and spirits were coming into union with His Spirit. James says that we should "in humility receive the word implanted, which is able to save your souls."[4] Our whole being needs to be saved: body, mind, emotions, and spirit. That's why we are to "receive the word implanted." It's the same idea as when Jesus said, "I am the vine, you are the branches; he who abides in Me and I in him, he bears much fruit, for apart from Me you can do nothing... If you abide in Me, and My words abide in you, ask whatever you wish, and it will be done for you."[5] We are to attach ourselves to the Word of God. As the psalmist says, we should hide God's Word in our hearts.[6]

This is "Christian Faith 101," the basic foundation: store up the Word of God in our hearts. Let Jesus feed us His Word. Then, let the wind of the Spirit blow upon His Word, and that wind will fan the flames of God's fire in our hearts. Our eyes will be opened and we will come into the knowledge of our glorious Messiah. We will also come into a place of intimate fellowship where we will break bread with Him and He with us. We will enjoy walking by His side, but there will also be times when He seems to disappear. If we protest that we can't see Him anymore, He will gently remind us that we walk by *faith*, and not by sight alone.

There's More to the Christian Life Than Just Catching Waves

The Lord wants a fire in us that will burn *within*, regardless of external circumstances. That's where some of us run into problems. I'm the type of person who wants to catch every wave of the Spirit that rolls in. I just want to get on my board and ride them all the way in. I'm sure many of you are the same way. We like to run off to wherever the "surf's up," and jump in. We go to this conference or that seminar, or we read the latest "revival" book. Catching waves is fun; it's exciting, refreshing, and exhilarating. The only problem is that there is much more to the Christian life than catching waves.

What about the times when there *are* no waves? What do we do when the sea is becalmed? That's when we go back to the foundations of "Christian Faith 101." Waves come and go, but God's Word stands forever, a sure foundation no matter what the weather. It's easy to become "external anointing junkies," whose spiritual health and vigor depend on the next conference or seminar "fix." When that happens, we tend to forget the basics of learning to walk in the internal anointing implanted in our hearts. We need to learn how to live out of the continual anointing of the Lord's presence from *within. This* is the walk of faith. It depends for life not on the changing waves that roll in but on the artesian spring that bubbles up constantly from the Rock that dwells within us: the Lord Jesus Christ. Consider Paul's words in Ephesians:

> *For this reason I bow my knees before the Father, from whom every family in heaven and on earth derives its name, that He would grant you, according to the riches of His glory, to be* **strengthened with power through His Spirit in the inner man, so that Christ may dwell in your hearts through faith***; and that you, being rooted and grounded in love, may be able to comprehend with all the saints what is the breadth and length and height and depth, and to know the love of Christ which surpasses knowledge,* **that you may be filled up to all the fullness of God.**[7]

Our Father's desire is that we be strengthened "in the inner man" by the presence of Christ in our hearts. Since Christ is Himself the "fullness of Deity...in bodily form,"[8] when He inhabits our hearts we are "filled up to all the fullness of God." As we learn to yield to His Lordship in humility and obedience, that fullness will overflow and spread to those around us. The live coals of fire in our hearts will flare up into a blaze that we cannot contain inside. It will be like what Jeremiah felt when he wrote, "But if I say, 'I will not remember Him/ Or speak anymore in His name,' / Then in my heart it becomes like a burning fire / Shut up in my bones; / And I am weary of holding it in / And I cannot endure it."[9]

We Are Called to Be Carriers of the Fire

The Lord has called us to be carriers of His fire—His presence. Paul said that the great mystery of the ages is Christ *in us,* the hope of glory.[10] There can be no greater manifestation of the Spirit than Christ living His life *in* and *through* us.

We have to pass through the outer court, as it were, and into the inner court to get the internal fire that we will carry back out to the world. We enter through the doorway of confession and repentance, where we are cleansed by the blood of Jesus at the brazen altar. Then we wash at the laver of God's Word, allowing it to transform us by the renewing of our minds so that we can prove what is the good, the acceptable, and the perfect will of God.[11] Proceeding to the golden lampstand, we are "lit up" with the brilliance of the anointing and gifting of the Spirit. Beyond is the table of shewbread, where the bread of the body of Jesus is laid out. We commune with Him there in intimate fellowship, then advance to the altar of incense, where we "pick up" the live coals of fire mingled with the incense of the prayers of the saints. Finally, when all is ready, we move beyond the veil into the Most Holy Place, the innermost "mansion" of our hearts where the Lord Himself dwells. The mingling of the fire in the firepan with the incense of the prayers of the saints creates the smoke of His presence. The Lord is there, and He communes with us.

The old Ark of the Covenant contained the tablets of the Law (God's Word), a pot of manna (God's provision—Jesus the Bread of Life), and Aaron's rod that budded (God's authority). What's inside *your* ark? Have you stored up in your ark any of the Word of God that the Holy Spirit can blow upon and make into a revelatory presence? Store up His Word. Call forth the divine wind of illumination to fan the flames. Fire warms, lights up, and purifies. As the fire burns within our hearts, it imparts to us the spirit of illumination and revelation. The fire sanctifies and empowers us.

As Brother Lawrence said, we need to *practice* the presence of God daily. We should *never* try to do anything in public or "on the platform" that we don't practice in private. Anyone who does needs to be delivered from a "performance spirit." There's an entertainment spirit that has permeated western Christianity. We're good "performers," but we have not been good maintainers of the inward fire. It's time for us to go forth and reclaim the inward journey, because in the long term we will be only as successful in the outward journey as we are in maintaining the inward fire.

The Lord Is Looking to See If We Have a Fire Within

Not long ago I had a powerful encounter with the Lord while participating in a Catch the Fire Conference in Birmingham, England. I was scheduled to speak one morning, and the night before, I stayed back from the main assembly so I could spend time alone with God. For three hours that night I lay on my bed, quietly praying in the gift of tongues and communing with my Lord, spirit to Spirit.

During that time, I heard the Lord say to me, "I am coming to see if there is any fire on your altar." That was a little scary to me.

After all, I had written about this and taught it. I had loved it and tried to impart it to others. Now the Lord Himself was saying to me, "I'm going to do a house inspection and see if there is anything more than just talk and revelation and gifts."

Then it was as though I underwent a spiritual "cat-scan." I felt the presence of God begin at my feet and slowly move up my body, penetrating my entire body until it stopped right over my heart. At that point the Lord graciously allowed me to see what He was seeing. On the altar of my heart there were hot burning coals of fire. Then He said to me, "I commission you to give away these coals of living fire that I have given to you, and you must teach My people how to maintain the fire within."

There's a fireplace in Papa's house (that's us), and He's looking to see if there is a fire there. If you've ever had a good fireplace in your home, you know how enjoyable it is to cozy up to the fire and sit there in quietness, possibly with a friend or your spouse, and just watch the wood burn and listen to it crackling. It's an atmosphere where you can let your guard down, share your most intimate secrets, and enjoy greater union with your companion. The Lord is our companion, and He's looking to see if there is a fire within. He wants there to be a place in our hearts where we can be warm with Him and where He can satisfy our soul. He wants passionate fire burning in our hearts!

We Need to Return to the Road to Emmaus

I remember one time doing a prayer tour in Israel with my wife and with our dear friend Avner Bosky, who heads the Israel-based ministry Final Frontiers. While we were there, Avner took us to places where the typical tours do not go—to some of the less traveled paths. Avner had no idea of the depth of my love for the 24th chapter of Luke, yet one of the places he took us to was the road to Emmaus. What a blessing it was to walk the same literal road that Jesus and those two disciples walked two thousand years ago!

At the same time, I felt a conviction and burden in my spirit, because today, the road to Emmaus is an uncared-for, weed-overgrown, and hilly path that few people travel anymore. In the natural, it describes the need today for the Body of Christ to return to the Emmaus of the burning fire within. It is a long-neglected path that needs to be restored.

It is the path where Jesus comes alongside and walks with us, sharing His Word and opening His heart to us. It is the path where we meditate upon the written Word of God and reflect upon the living Word of God who dwells in our hearts. As I walked along that road to Emmaus, I pondered how the hearts of those disciples who met Jesus were burning within them. It broke my heart and I wept before the Lord.

Our loving Father and gracious Lord wants *our* hearts to burn within just like those disciples of old. He wants our hearts to beat in synchronous rhythm with His own; to feel as He feels, sorrow as He sorrows, rejoice as He rejoices, and love as He loves. His heart burns for us to take the living coals of fire in our hearts and place them upon others at their exact points of pain and brokenness, so the cleansing purity of His love and grace can cauterize their wounds and bring healing, deliverance, and redemption.

Just as the coal of fire from Heaven's altar touched Isaiah's lips, cleansed him inside and out, and ignited a flame in his heart that would never go out, so the Lord wants to touch us. He wants to take that same coal of fire and set our hearts ablaze in a white-hot passion for Him that will consume us totally, yet preserve us in perfect union with Him.

The Fire of His Love

The inward is for the outward, and the living fire on the altar of our heart is the fuel that will propel us from the warmth of our own personal Emmaus into the dark and downtrodden, harried and hopeless ways and byways of a lost and hurting world. We are a drink offering for our Lord, poured out and wasted for Him, just as the pure nard with which Mary of Bethany anointed the feet of Jesus. *Let the fire burn brightly!*

Let's follow in the paths of those who have gone before us. Practice the presence of God like Brother Lawrence. Enroll with Christ in the school of prayer like Andrew Murray. Learn there are many rooms to fill in our Father's house—like St. Teresa. Walk in the footsteps of Joshua in meditative prayer. Be consumed with the fire of love by entering into the bridegroom's fast and join Anna the praying prophetess.

But just give your all to Him! Do not hold back. Be extravagant in your reach for Him. After all, isn't He worth it?!

With Holy yearnings, this is my epistle of passion written to you!

Reflection Questions

1. The angel took live coals of fire from the altar and touched them to Isaiah's lips. What was the result?

2. In the Old Testament, where did the coals of fire rest? Which station and where?

3. If God came to inspect your temple, what would He find on the altar of your heart?

Recommended Reading

The Lost Art of Intercession by Jim W. Goll (Destiny Image, 1997)

Why Revival Tarries by Leonard Ravenhill (Bethany House Publishers, 1982)

Fire on the Altar by Jim W. Goll (Ministry to the Nations, 1996)

Endnotes

1. Is. 6:1-8.
2. Lk. 24:13-16.
3. Lk. 24:27-32.
4. Jas. 1:21b.
5. Jn. 15:5, 7.
6. See Ps. 119:11.
7. Eph. 3:14-19, emphasis added.
8. Col. 2:9b.
9. Jer. 20:9.
10. See Col. 1:26-27.
11. See Rom. 12:2.

For More Information

Jim Goll and his wife, Michal Ann, are founders of Ministry to the Nations, an organization based in Franklin, Tennessee, dedicated to releasing God's presence through prophetic intercession, missions, and training.

After pastoring for thirteen years, Jim was thrust forth in 1987 into an itinerant role of equipping leaders and churches. He has traveled extensively across North, Central, and South America, Europe, Asia, the former Soviet Union, Israel and the Caribbean, teaching and imparting the power of intercession, prophetic ministry, and life in the Holy Spirit. Jim was a teacher at the School of the Spirit of the Grace Training Center, Kansas City, Missouri, and a dean of Christian Leadership University, Buffalo, New York. He is presently an instructor with the Wagner Leadership Institute.

Jim and Michal Ann's other books include: *The Lost Art of Intercession; Encounters With a Supernatural God; Women on the Front Lines; Kneeling on the Promises; Fire on the Altar; Father, Forgive Us!* and three study guides. Jim has recorded an audio condensed version of *The Lost Art of Intercession* and *Prayers for Israel*, both on cassette and CD. All of these products are available from their website.

He and Michal Ann have been married for twenty-four years and have four children. They reside in Franklin, Tennessee.

For more information:

Jim W. Goll
Ministry to the Nations
P.O. Box 1653
Franklin, TN 37065
Office Phone: **(615) 599-5552**
Office Fax: **(615) 599-5554**
e-mail: **MTTN155550@aol.com**
Websites: **http://www.ministrytothenations.org**
Or **www.JimGoll.com**

Books to help you grow strong in Jesus

➤ FATHER, FORGIVE US!

by Jim W. Goll.

What is holding back a worldwide "great awakening"? What hinders the Church all over the world from rising up and bringing in the greatest harvest ever known? The answer is simple: sin! God is calling Christians today to take up the mantle of identificational intercession and repent for the sins of the present and past; for the sins of our fathers; for the sins of the nations. Will you heed the call? This book shows you how!

ISBN 0-7684-2025-3

➤ THE LOST ART OF INTERCESSION

by Jim W. Goll.

Finally there is something that really explains what is happening to so many folk in the Body of Christ. What does it mean to carry the burden of the Lord? Where is it in Scripture and in history? Why do I feel as though God is groaning within me? No, you are not crazy; God is restoring genuine intercessory prayer in the hearts of those who are open to respond to His burden and His passion.

ISBN 1-56043-697-2

➤ ENCOUNTERS WITH A SUPERNATURAL GOD

by Jim W. and Michal Ann Goll.

The Golls know that angels are real. They have firsthand experience with supernatural angelic encounters. In this book you'll read and learn about angels and supernatural manifestations of God's Presence—and the real encounters that both Jim and Michal Ann have had! As the founders of Ministry to the Nations and speakers and teachers, they share that God wants to be intimate friends with His people. Go on an adventure with the Golls and find out if God has a supernatural encounter for you!

ISBN 1-56043-199-7

➤ WOMEN ON THE FRONT LINES

by Michal Ann Goll.

History is filled with ordinary women who have changed the course of their generation. Here Michal Ann Goll, co-founder of Ministry to the Nations with her husband, Jim, shares how her own life was transformed and highlights nine women whose lives will impact yours! Every generation faces the same choices and issues; learn how you, too, can heed the call to courage and impact a generation.

ISBN 0-7684-2020-2

Available at your local Christian bookstore.

For more information and sample chapters, visit www.reapernet.com

Books to help you grow strong in Jesus

➤ SECRET SOURCES OF POWER

by T.F. Tenney with Tommy Tenney.

Everyone is searching for power. People are longing for some external force to empower their lives and transform their circumstances. *Secret Sources of Power* furnishes some of the keys that will unlock the door to Divine power. You might be surprised at what is on the other side of that door. It will be the opposite of the world's concepts of power and how to obtain it. You will discover that before you lay hold of God's power you must let go of your own resources. You will be challenged to go down before you can be lifted up. Death always comes before resurrection. If you are dissatisfied with your life and long for the power of God to be manifested in you then now is the time. Take the keys and open the door to *Secret Sources of Power*!

ISBN 0-7684-5000-4

➤ THE GOD CHASERS (National Best-Seller)

by Tommy Tenney.

There are those so hungry, so desperate for His presence, that they become consumed with finding Him. Their longing for Him moves them to do what they would otherwise never do: Chase God. But what does it really mean to chase God? Can He be "caught"? Is there an end to the thirsting of man's soul for Him? Meet Tommy Tenney—God chaser. Join him in his search for God. Follow him as he ignores the maze of religious tradition and finds himself, not chasing God, but to his utter amazement, caught by the One he had chased.

ISBN 0-7684-2016-4

Also available in Spanish

ISBN 0-7899-0642-2

➤ GOD CHASERS DAILY MEDITATION & PERSONAL JOURNAL

by Tommy Tenney.

ISBN 0-7684-2040-7

➤ GOD'S FAVORITE HOUSE

by Tommy Tenney.

The burning desire of your heart can be fulfilled. God is looking for people just like you. He is a Lover in search of a people who will love Him in return. He is far more interested in you than He is interested in a building. He would hush all of Heaven's hosts to listen to your voice raised in heartfelt love songs to Him. This book will show you how to build a house of worship within, fulfilling your heart's desire and His!

ISBN 0-7684-2043-1

➤ THE LOST PASSIONS OF JESUS

by Donald L. Milam, Jr.

What motivated Jesus to pursue the cross? What inner strength kept His feet on the path laid before Him? Time and tradition have muted the Church's knowledge of the passions that burned in Jesus' heart, but if we want to—if we dare to—we can still seek those same passions. Learn from a close look at Jesus' own life and words and from the writings of other dedicated followers the passions that enflamed the Son of God and changed the world forever!

ISBN 0-9677402-0-7

Available at your local Christian bookstore.

Exciting titles
by Don Nori